Climbing the
Rainbow

Climbing the
Rainbow

Kathleen M. Wandishin

Book design by Launch My Book, Inc (www.launchmybook.com) with cover design by Erika Alyana Duran (easduran.myportfolio.com) and interior design by Booknook.biz.

Published in the United States of America by Kathleen M. Wandishin.

Identifiers:
ISBN 979-8-9919174-0-7 (Paperback)
ISBN 979-8-9919174-1-4 (Ebook)

I dedicate this labor of love to my family—Jim, my loving husband, Christine and Katie—my beautiful daughters, and Joseph, Stephen and John—my equally beautiful sons. They were my steadfast companions on this most difficult journey, and as we clung to one another through it all, we discovered that our family is an extraordinary gift to each of us!

Contents

Introduction

I HAVE LIVED THROUGH many difficult, heartbreaking, and tragic events in my life, as you will read in this book. When I tell my story, the listener almost always asks: "How are you even standing right now? How are you not a crumbled piece of humanity hiding under the covers?" I answer them, "Because I have learned two very important responses when I am faced with a difficult trial: to truly trust God and be open to the authentic truth I will learn from living it." Because I have been able to trust God completely with everything in my life and I have worked very hard at opening my mind to the possible lesson I might learn, I have become a completely different version of myself than I ever thought possible. At first, I encountered each of these events in my life reluctantly and with my feet dug firmly in. I felt broken, defeated, and hopeless. I felt abandoned by God, whom I have served faithfully all my life. I couldn't believe this was my life and raged against God, asking Him, "Could you just give me a break?" I would utter often to myself and to my close friends, "I hate my life." But as time went on and I navigated through each challenge, I made a conscious effort to open my mind to what God was teaching me through each trial. As I received insight into a new idea or thought about life, I wrote about it. This book is a collection of many of the life-changing events in my life and the life lesson I learned from each one. I firmly believe that without the experiences I have suffered through, I would not be who I am today. I am genuinely happy. I am peaceful. I am confident in the person I have become. I do not fear change or the possibility of future tribulations or losses. I have heard from the media and random people that "the world is on fire," based on the events of the last five to ten years. Yes, there are many terrible things going on in the world right now, but I refuse to buy into the doom-and-gloom attitude. I pray constantly and place the world in God's hands, and I let it go. There is very little I can do about these huge world problems, but God can, and I ask Him to. In all things, I know that God has wrapped His ever-loving arms around me and will bring me through whatever burden faces me with a renewed understanding and appreciation of His greater plan for me.

I accept that life is difficult, and I face each day with the expected promise that I will learn something important, an essential truth that will aid me as I continue my unique journey in life. I believe that God created each of us for a specific purpose. No one else ever created or to be created can fulfill the dream God has for each of us. Each day I live, I am joyful knowing that I am becoming the person God created me to be.

Each chapter in this book is a description of an event or a day or timeframe during an event and my feelings about what was happening to me. After each chapter, I explain the life lesson or truth that I learned from living through this incident or occurrence.

My goal is twofold. I have been thinking about writing this manuscript for twenty years. First, I want to honor my son, John, who suffered for five and a half years from leukemia and died the day before his sixteenth birthday. In fact, one of the accomplishments he had on his bucket list was to write a book about his cancer journey. John taught me so much about the true purpose of life. But my life didn't get any easier after his death. As I was plunged into more trials for almost two decades after his passing, I started to realize the many life truths I was able to accumulate in my knowledge of myself and God. I traveled closer and closer to understanding the age-old questions that everyone has asked at some time in their lives: "Why are we here?" and "What is our purpose?" And so, my second reason for sharing these stories is to impart the simple yet profound awareness I have gained that might be able to help you navigate the tribulations in your life. My hope is that you will read something that resonates with you and gives you the power, courage, and confident hope to face the current or future trial that may await you, and possibly fill you with anticipated wonder about the possible discoveries you may find as you journey through life.

CHAPTER 1

The Day My Life Changed Forever

"THIS DISEASE can be cured." Those words were the only ones I could focus on that day of February 16, 2000. The very young-looking doctor with curly red hair and freckles and wearing a novelty tie, one of the kind that pediatricians always wear to help put kids at ease but really doesn't work anyway, just told my husband Jim and I that our ten-year-old son had acute myeloid leukemia. He had just performed a bone marrow aspiration on my son John and had called us to the small conference room to give us the results. We would later dub it the "doom and gloom" room since that's where family members and parents were called in to receive serious news. You knew if you were called in there, it wasn't going to be good. "He will need a bone marrow transplant," Dr. Jeff was saying. I remember thinking, how can he know? He doesn't look old enough to be a doctor who would know life-and-death kind of stuff. Dr. Jeff went on to explain that the rest of our four children would be tested to see if any of them could be a match for John's marrow. While we were waiting for those results, John would be immediately admitted to the hospital and would have surgery the next day to place a central line in his chest that would serve as access for chemotherapy. Then, after more thorough testing was done on his marrow to determine what protocol would work best with his type of cancer, chemo would be started. John would probably be in the hospital for about three weeks. Three weeks! I couldn't comprehend being away from home for that long—the longest we had ever been away from our house and animals was our yearly one-week stay at Ocean City.

I suddenly felt a huge weight of guilt fall upon me. I asked Dr. Jeff, "Did we do anything to cause this? Did we wait too long to bring him in?" My mind was racing, thinking of John's childhood and any possible event or mothering error that could have made this happen. He had been suffering from a respiratory illness for several months. His doctor diagnosed him with mild bronchitis. He had suffered dozens of respiratory infections, as well as throat and ear infections during his childhood, not unlike any of his siblings. Kids just get sick a lot. But he had been fighting this infection since before Christmas. A course of antibiotics would make him better, and as soon as he finished taking the medicine, he would get sick again. But this happened quite a lot, too. Most of my kids needed at least two courses of amoxicillin or a higher-potency drug to knock the bug out of them. I really hadn't thought much about it.

But then we noticed the fatigue. John was an extremely active kid with lots of energy to burn. He was constantly going full speed, running around the house pretending to be his favorite superhero and yelling at the top of his lungs. He was once caught whacking our neighbor's new crepe myrtle bush with a stick, pretending it was a dragon that needed slaying. It eventually grew up to be a beautiful tree, but at that time, I was sure I would be going to the nursery to buy Susan another one. As a toddler, he was constantly getting into stuff, taking things apart to satisfy his curiosity about how it worked. He never wanted to go to bed at night; he was too busy playing and discovering his world. John was the youngest of five children, and I am sure he felt that he had to be loud and boisterous to make sure he was noticed. Sometimes he was just plain annoying, and I longed for bedtime to get a reprieve from the constant activity. So, when John started coming home from school and just wanted to sleep or lay around, I became a little suspicious. I assumed it was the bronchitis he was battling, but it did seem to be an awfully long time that he had been suffering from it. Then we noticed that at his basketball games he would barely run up the court and would become winded, begging the coach to take him out. John was very athletic, playing organized sports year-round—soccer in the fall and spring and basketball in the winter. He was quite good, and his coaches played him frequently. But his becoming tired so soon into the game was unusual.

The bruising was the ultimate sign for me that something was wrong. I observed bruises on his knuckles and between his fingers. He always had bruises up and down his legs, as all little boys do when they play hard. But these were unusual places for him to sustain enough injury to cause a bruise. At the same time, I noticed that he no longer had his delightful rosy cheeks and happy grin. His color was sallow, almost gray, and he rarely smiled any more. I made an appointment to take him to the pediatrician that week.

Valentine's Day was cold and gray that year. The kids all had their little valentine surprises at their places on the table when they awoke and then went off to school, and I went to work. I worked at my church's office, which was just across the driveway from the parish school. It served as a great arrangement. We all left the house together and all came home together. And I was always close by in case one of the children needed something. At the end of that day, we had a dinner that everyone loved, and we settled down to watch some TV before going to bed. The older children were watching *The Bachelor* and the younger ones were reading the valentines they had received at school that day. All except John. He was lying on the couch and complaining that his shoulder hurt. The pain continued to worsen until he was literally crying in pain. I thought that maybe he had slept on it weirdly the night before or injured it at recess that day in school. I gave him some Tylenol and tried to console him. He slept fitfully and still complained of pain in the morning. I called the pediatrician's office and asked if I could bring him in that day instead of waiting for my appointment. I got an appointment a little later in the day and took John to work with me so he could lie on the couch in the living room of the rectory.

When we arrived at the doctor's office, we had to see a doctor on the "adult" side, since none of the pediatricians were in. John was uncomfortable and continued to cry on and off because of the pain. I explained John's symptoms to the doctor, and she examined him. She told him she had to take a blood sample and then asked me to go into another room for a moment. There she told me that she would be testing for leukemia and lymphoma. I remember thinking that this was just a precaution. Surely it wouldn't be anything like that. There was probably some simple explanation for John's symptoms and a concoction of medicine would fix him right up. She told me to call her tomorrow afternoon for the results.

I took John home and tried to make him comfortable. I phoned Jim at work and told him what the doctor had said and then I called my mother. We all agreed that it was probably something simple. We couldn't imagine him having some kind of cancer. It was inconceivable and only happened to other people.

The next morning, I went to work and again brought John along. My desk phone rang at 8:15 a.m. that morning. It was the doctor John had seen yesterday. She said that his blood tests were very abnormal and rattled off a string of numbers that didn't mean anything to me. She said that she had already made an appointment for us at the University of Maryland Oncology and Hematology Department for Children for 12:00 noon that day. She said they were expecting us. I hung up the phone and my mind went numb. Oncology department? Surely this must be some mistake. Oncology means cancer. Why were they sending us there? I knew what the words meant. I couldn't get my heart and my mind to comprehend.

I called my friend Dot and asked her if she could go with me. I didn't even know how to get to the University of Maryland! Dot and I had become fast friends in a really short time. She was the youth minister at our Catholic church, and we worked closely together. Since all four of my other children were teens at that time, I volunteered often to assist her with activities for the youth, much to my kids' opposition. We hit it off famously and had great fun together as well as sharing our most intimate thoughts and feelings. The greatest test of our friendship had come in August of the previous year. Dot's only daughter was killed in an automobile accident. Kelly, just eighteen years old and graduated from high school, was killed instantly on Route 70 on her way to see her boyfriend. I was on a family vacation at the time at the beach when she called to tell me. I immediately packed up my family and came home to be with her. Those following days and weeks were unimaginably painful. Her devastation was raw and bloody, and I clung to her, ever ready to mop up the blood and dress her gaping wounds. I couldn't think of a worse horror than to lose your child. As I walked so intimately with her sorrow, I saw much more closely than I wanted to how broken and bereft you become when your baby dies. I saw her own wish for death and her lack of desire to live without her child. I saw how grief consumed her like a hungry lion, leaving nothing but dry, flesh-picked bones. I could only imagine the emptiness of her existence—the huge, groaning hole that was left of her heart. I grieved with her. I loved her with everything I had to help her see her way through her darkness. And I was relieved that it hadn't happened to me.

Dot drove John and me to the hospital. She dropped us off at the main doors and went to park the car. When we walked in, I immediately became disoriented. It was like a small city. The entire front of the hospital was a large atrium, one entire wall sporting windows that let the sun in, creating bright patches on the floor. There were lots of people walking about, all hurrying to some part of the hospital. John was whimpering because his shoulder hurt and had a hard time walking. I had no idea where we were going and headed down a hallway. I must have looked frantic because a kind nurse asked if she could help me. I told her where we needed to go, and she pointed me to the elevators that would take us up to the fifth floor in the children's wing. As I turned from the elevator I saw the door. The sign painted on it said Children's Foundation Oncology and Hematology Department. My heart pounded in my chest as I opened the door, and I somehow got the feeling that I would be spending a lot of time there.

As soon as we walked in, someone at the front desk asked if this was John Wandishin. When I said yes, she smiled and said, "We have been expecting you. Come, let's get you comfortable." We were ushered into a small examination room and John lay on the table. Soon, we were surrounded by a nurse (Chrissy), a child life specialist (Dawn), and Dr. Jeff. The nurse was trying to establish an IV in John's arm, but his vein kept collapsing. "This happens a lot when kids are this sick," she said. This sick? There it was again; a reference that we weren't dealing with something easy. John was screaming and thrashing about. It took both Dot and I to hold him still. After Chrissy managed to get a needle in, she gave him a drug to help him relax and manage his pain. Dr. Jeff explained to us that he needed to perform a bone marrow aspiration to harvest some of his marrow so that it could be examined at the lab and a diagnosis could be made. He asked if my husband was here. I told him he was at work. Jim was a letter carrier, and it was often difficult to get in touch with him while he was on the route. Dr. Jeff told me gently that I should make every effort to talk to him and get him to the hospital. Dot got out her cell phone and immediately called the post office. In her no-nonsense way, she demanded that they find Jim wherever he was and tell him to come up to the University of Maryland. They assured her that they would find him and deliver the message.

The procedure was explained to John in simple detail so he could understand. He barely listened. He just wanted to stop hurting. He was taken into the procedure room and given another IV drug to put him in twilight sleep. I was assured that he wouldn't feel or remember anything. John was placed on his belly and Dr. Jeff prepared to stick the biggest, thickest needle I had ever seen into my son's hip. I sat at John's head and whispered what a brave boy he was being. As the needle plunged deep into John's hip bone, he screamed. I was unnerved. He wasn't supposed to feel this. Dr. Jeff again said he wouldn't remember any of this, but John continued to cry and move his head from side to side. His eyes were closed, and I could tell he wasn't coherent, but still he felt it, even if he never remembered it. I vowed that if he had to go through this procedure again, he would have full-fledged anesthesia; no more of this so-called twilight stuff. It was too heartbreaking to see him hurt. Finally, enough marrow was harvested, and John was wheeled into another quiet room to recover and sleep. The medical team suggested to Dot that she take me downstairs to get something to eat. It would take a while before John woke up and they would have the lab results.

We went down to the atrium and found Donna's Café. It was an upscale, trendy sandwich place. The menu listed unusual and creative choices. I had never heard of most of them. Lots of sprouts, mushrooms, and goat cheese. I don't remember what I ordered; something with chicken, I think. I wasn't hungry at all, and my stomach was too tied up in knots to eat. But to humor Dot, I ordered a sandwich, if not just to look at and move around a few times. While we were sitting at a table in the atrium, Father Sam found us. Fr. Sam was the interim pastor of the parish at which I worked and my kids went to school. We had just bade our last pastor, Father Mike, farewell that previous Sunday as he had been assigned to a new parish. This had been a difficult and emotional time for me. Mike and I worked well together and had become good friends. I was very sad to see him move on and apprehensive to meet my new boss. It just so happened that Fr. Sam's first day at the parish was today. I literally said hello to him that morning and goodbye a few hours later as I headed up to the hospital. I certainly didn't make a very good impression on him as to what kind of employee I was. As his administrative assistant, it would be essential for me to fill him in on the workings of the parish, show him the procedures and how things had been done, give him a glimpse of the flavor and personality of the parishioners, and serve as historian of the time before he came. I never missed time and gave 110% on the job. I am of German heritage and we Germans are very hard workers and possess an impeccable work ethic. Now on his very first day with his new staff, I had left the office, and it looked like I would be gone for a while. I would be little help to him as he became familiar with his new post. However, I was moved and comforted by the fact that he had come to the hospital to be with me. The first days at a new job are challenging. All is new and unfamiliar and there is much to learn. Yet, Sam left it all to comfort me.

After staring at my sandwich for a while, it was time to go back up to the oncology department. Jim had found his way to the hospital and was waiting for us. We were told to wait a few minutes, and then ushered into the "room." There we were told of John's diagnosis. He had acute myeloid leukemia, simply known as AML. The kind doctor assured me that nothing I had done or not done had caused John to have this disease. There was still no theory as to why leukemia attacked.

I sat there hearing all these words but not really understanding them. I felt like I was in some movie, and this was one of those gut-wrenching scenes that make even men cry. It was like this was happening to someone else. This couldn't be my son he was talking about. This couldn't be my life that was about to be irrevocably changed. This stuff only happened to other people. I always felt badly for them and was secretly and immensely relieved that it wasn't me. I would bake them a casserole and send them a card and maybe babysit their other children. But now, I was on the other side. This really bad thing was happening to me and my family. There was no reference point or prior experience to help me chart the way. I was not in control any longer. It wouldn't be as simple as just cooking a meal for someone and saying grateful prayers that my children were healthy. My thoughts were interrupted as Dr. Jeff said we should all go into the recovery room where John was coming out of the anesthesia and tell him. As I walked out of the room, I wondered, how do you tell a ten-year-old child that he has a deadly disease?

He cried. I was worried that John didn't understand all that this illness and its treatment would require of him. But he knew more than I thought he did. His fifth-grade class was doing a service project for the Leukemia Society and was raising money. To help them better understand what their charity did, his class watched a film about the disease. Snoopy and the Peanuts gang explained the disease and its symptoms and described the treatment necessary to cure it. As soon as we told him what was wrong with him, he remembered the film and knew exactly what it was. But I doubt he knew enough to understand that his life was about to change forever. That he would battle it for years to come. That the hospital would become his second home. That everything he did would be in the shadow of AML. That he would cheat death a dozen times and come back each time to continue the battle. That he would become an inspiration to many and would change the way others looked at life and its challenges. It's good he didn't know all that then. It was a blessing that Jim and I didn't either.

After Dr. Jeff explained to John what was going to happen next, it was time to go to the room that would be our home for the next seven weeks. Dawn, the child life specialist and certified angel, gave him a stuffed TY raccon that would become his constant companion for the rest of his treatment. John had come into the hospital in a good deal of pain, and it was obvious he needed some relief. So off he went, rolling in his bed down the hall to his room. Jim and I stayed back for a few minutes so the nurses could get him settled. Dr. Jeff told us to give each other a hug and allow the tears to come. We would need each other's strength and comfort for the long months ahead. But the tears didn't come. We were like robots, mechanically embracing and then following John back to his room. The fog of disbelief and shock was thick and soupy. Walking down that hall after this incredibly long day of unfamiliar surroundings and foreign medical terms was like walking in a tunnel. We couldn't see where we were going, we couldn't see any light, and we didn't know when we would get out of it.

CHAPTER 2

Without Change There Is No Growth

MOST PEOPLE DO NOT like change. We humans become easily comfortable in our familiar routines. We feel safe and secure in the knowledge of what we know. We might like a specific type of bread at our grocery store. Then one day we go to the store to buy it and it's not there. We ask a clerk and are told they no longer carry it and in fact, it's not being made any longer. Immediately we feel cheated and frustrated. Just when we find something we like and we become accustomed to it being available to us, in an instant it is taken away from us. There is no good substitute. I love the specific raisin bread that Geresbeck's supermarket bakes at their stores. It is a big part of my breakfast routine, and I will be quite vexed if they should stop baking it. Something as mundane as a type of bread or a brand of ice cream or a certain make of shoe becomes a loss when it's no longer available to us. And we must put forth the effort and time to find something else that would satisfy this need.

Today, as I write this on March 26, 2024, I woke up to the news that the Francis Scott Key Bridge had collapsed into the Patapsco River in Baltimore. I travel over this bridge almost every day to babysit my granddaughter so my daughter can go to work. I watched the video of the accident repeatedly. It was gone in three seconds. It was a shocking loss! Just last night I traveled over it on my way home. It was my lifeline to my granddaughter. Somehow now she seems much farther away from me. She still lives in the same place but my route to get to her will take much longer. Besides the enormous tragedy of lost lives, lost income and jobs, and families who will be forever mourning their loved ones, this is a tremendous change for many, many people who relied on that bridge every day.

Change is inevitable. It will continue to happen all our lives. Some changes are small, like not being able to buy the type of bread we like, and some will be huge and life-changing, like a medical diagnosis or loss of a loved one. But it is guaranteed to happen. And I have learned that change is essential—both good and tragic—for us to grow and to learn important life lessons. Without change, we stay stagnant and stuck, unable to move forward to embrace God's promise for us. Change in the sense of a loss like the bread you ate for breakfast, or your job, or your home, forces you into looking ahead for other choices, for a newer way, for a different solution that might even be better than the one you lost. We don't know what other good things are out there for us if we stay stuck in the same old choices and don't have a reason to seek something better.

For several decades of my early life, I did not like myself. I hated who I was. I dreamed of the characteristics that I should have to make me a better person. I wanted to be more patient, or more articulate when I spoke to others, or grateful for my blessings instead of complaining about what I lacked. I was too stuck in my low self-esteem to even have a clue how to attain these virtues. I was the firstborn in a devout Catholic household, the oldest of five. I wore my firstborn responsibility well, always listening to my parents, helping with the household chores, assisting my younger siblings, and being obedient. In school I was a straight-A student, respectful of my teachers and ever helpful in the classroom—helping put up bulletin boards, clapping erasers, or running errands. I was "teacher's pet" every year. In middle school and in the first years of high school, this behavior earned me the disdain of my fellow classmates. Kids hate the teacher's pet. I was cruelly bullied by my supposed girlfriends, left out of weekend parties and sleepovers, and called names. The girls who followed me in high school kept up this cruel behavior, whispering to each other about me, throwing my books and pencils all over the bus for me to retrieve, and ignoring me.

My decision to not indulge in using foul language, smoking, drinking alcohol, or "putting out" for the boys only solidified the fact that I was not worthy of the friendship from girls and boys alike. I was a "goody two-shoes" and unrelatable to most kids of the 1960s and 70s. I cried every afternoon when I got home, feeling completely alone. I did not have a friend in the world, especially when friends were so important to a girl my age. In my junior year of high school, I met Mary. She was just like me, held the same values dear, and made wise choices and we became the best of friends. To this day she is one of my dearest and closest friends in life. I was able to move on with Mary's friendship as my lifeline, but the damage had been done. It took years of therapy to finally come to the realization that I was valuable, that I mattered, and I had an important role in this world. I was treasured, loved, and cherished because I was God's child. I remember the afternoon in my therapist's office when this incredible insight exploded in my mind. It changed everything! And from then on, I looked for every opportunity to discover the unique and specially designed traits that made up who I was and who I was meant to be when God created me. These opportunities only came with changes, during the difficult times, and through the tears and questions and feelings of despair.

Most of us don't enjoy change. Change takes us out of our comfort zone and requires effort, energy, and prayer to find our way through it. It makes us move out of the familiar, the safe, and often the complacency of our lives. At this writing, the Archdiocese of Baltimore is proposing to close forty of their churches, one of them being my church. The congregations of these parishes will need to find another community to join. It is a tremendous loss for so many faithful parishioners. Many Catholics, including myself, are lifelong members of our parishes. We have grown up with these people. They are our extended family and have celebrated with us during our happy times and carried us through the worst times. I have known some of these people my entire life. This is a paramount loss for so many whose lives are about to change forever. I will not debate the reasons or events that have caused these drastic decisions, and I am feeling angry and downhearted. Some of these people I will never see again until I attend their funeral. But I realize, once again, that this coming change is granting me another opportunity to learn something import-ant. It will encourage me to find the blessing in it, and I admit that it will take a lot of patience and stepping outside of myself and my desires to find it. But I am completely confident that I will discover what God is teaching me through this most painful event.

I encourage you, as hard and as seemingly impossible as it might be, to learn to be open to change. Try to embrace the changes that come, whether they be small or monumental. The insights, clarity, understanding, and peace that await you when you get to the other side will surprise you!

CHAPTER 3

We Had Only Just Begun to Fight

THE FIRST NIGHT OF John's hospital admission was surreal. Although he was getting medication to alleviate his pain, he was very uncomfortable. When they placed the IV in his arm in the crook of his elbow, they bound his arm to a hard board to keep him from bending his elbow. He often woke up crying and complaining that his arm hurt from the needle and the board. I knew this was necessary to deliver the pain medication to him, but I ached to ease his suffering and felt so helpless that I couldn't relieve his pain. He was in a private room right outside of the helicopter pad. Many times during the next seven weeks, we would watch the big bird land and take off. It was an interesting distraction. The room had a long window seat that was just wide enough for a thin person to lay on. That's where I slept. Or didn't, for several nights. I never could sleep away from my bed at home. When we went on our summer vacation in Ocean City each year, I didn't sleep for the first two or three nights. Even though we rented the same condo every year and it was in a sense our home away from home, sleep still evaded me for the first few nights. As soon as I felt comfortable enough to sleep through the night it was usually time to go home! The thought of spending at least three weeks sleeping on this skinny vinyl pad where, every time I rolled over, I woke up trying to ensure I wouldn't fall off onto the floor, was unimaginable. The longest I had been away from home was one week. Dr. Jeff told us that if all went well, we would be able to go home in three weeks.

Dot, Sister Marianne (a trusted work colleague and friend), and my dear friend Diana joined forces and gathered up my four older children—Christine, my oldest in her first year of college; Joseph, my oldest son in his senior year of high school; Stephen, my middle son in his freshman year of high school; and Katie, my fourth child who was an eighth grader in middle school—and explained John's diagnosis to them and what was going to happen. They were shocked and concerned and, as teenagers who are usually heavily involved in their own self-discovery, worried about how this would affect them. Dot and Diana packed a bag for me so that I would have clean clothes and toiletries for the next several weeks, and Jim brought it up. As I lay fitfully trying to wrap my head around this enormous thing that had happened to us, I could not pray. I could not untangle the mess of thoughts in my head, and I could not sleep. This was huge and I was in shock.

The next day, John was prepped for surgery of his chest port placement. It would be a double lumen Hickman catheter consisting of two tubes that were inserted directly into a vein in his chest. It was through these tubes that chemo would be delivered and any medication that could not be taken by mouth. This was an invaluable tool for the medical team and for John, as he would need many, many medications and blood products delivered intravenously over the next months, and it was a painless way to accomplish this. There would be weeks ahead when John couldn't keep any food or liquid down from the side effects of chemo, and knowing he could still receive his medication was a huge comfort. Before we went home, I would have to learn how to clean the area each day, redress it, and flush the tubes with saline and heparin. To this day I am still amazed at what I had to learn during the next several years to care for John. I jokingly referred to it as "crash course nursing."

During that first couple of days, we were overwhelmed with information. We were given a huge binder of information that explained John's disease, its symptoms, and its treatment. Every time a new drug was given, we were given a paper that explained the medicine, what it did, and its side effects. We were visited by a social worker who explained to us some of the resources that were available to help us navigate this journey. She also gave us lots of information to read that gave us some idea what the next several months would look like. We were encouraged to share our feelings about what we were experiencing, our fears and our needs. We applied for discounted parking vouchers. Being in the city, the only parking available to us was an underground garage, and it was expensive to park there for the day, much less several weeks. We signed up to receive discounted vouchers to use in the hospital cafeteria. Most people don't realize that a serious illness that will require lengthy hospital stays can truly strain your finances. Suddenly you are putting out funds for food, parking, gasoline, and necessities that weren't needed before. We filled out applications to Believe in Tomorrow (formerly known as Grant a Wish) and Casey Cares, which were and still are local organizations that specialize in granting sick kids and their families new experiences, trips, and parties, as well as vouchers for pizza, entertainment, and fun outings—things that any family going through this ordeal could not afford. We applied to the Make a Wish Foundation, the national charity that grants desperately sick children a big wish, whether it be a trip, meeting a celebrity, or going to a special event. These organizations were life-giving and enormously instrumental in helping to make a very bad situation more bearable.

The hospital chaplain came to see us and tried to attend to our spiritual needs and questions. I say tried because I remember being very resistant to anything he had to say. I was a devout Catholic and raising our children in the Church. At the time of John's diagnosis, I was also working for my parish as the office administrator. I had been a rule follower all my life and I was a good Catholic, never missing Mass and making sure the kids received all their sacraments. I went to my wedding night a virgin, and Jim and I practiced natural family planning according to Church teaching. You might think, "Well, that sure didn't work—five kids!" But each child was planned and wanted. I did everything right. Why had God allowed this to happen to us? I was angry. Angry at the situation, but mostly with God. I couldn't pray and I didn't want to. I had held up my part of the bargain and lived my life according to His Church. What had I done to deserve this unspeakable trial? I was also in denial. Surely there had been a terrible mistake made and they would come into our room any minute to let us know

John had something much less sinister. When a well-meaning priest from my aunt's parish came to visit and asked if he could pray with me, I politely allowed him to pray for John, but I wanted to take no part in it. John didn't need these prayers. He wasn't that sick. It was all a mistake. Denial is a common coping mechanism. It makes you feel better for a while, but sooner or later reality will hit hard, and you are only temporarily avoiding the inevitable truth.

The kids, Dot, and Diana came to visit on the second evening. John's surgery had gone well, his pain was being better managed, and chemo was slated to start later that night. I was antsy and nervous. I thought I might explode from my pent-up emotions. I had been stoic for the last thirty-six hours, not wanting to show my emotion in front of John. I didn't want to scare him, and I wanted to be strong so he could be strong. I was his mom. I had to be able to comfort him and allay his fears. He looked to me to protect him, to wipe his tears and soothe his pain. When everyone arrived that evening, I could barely contain my tears. I took one look at Dot and Diana and said I had to take a walk. My face contorted in an anguished cry, and they quickly led me to the chapel. There they held me as the sobs erupted from the deepest of places in me. Time stood still as all the fears, sadness, and anger spilled forth from my eyes, my nose, and my mouth. No one said anything. They just held me and I ugly-cried. There was nothing to be said. It was every parent's nightmare. It was the biggest, baddest, ugliest, scariest thing that could ever happen. My baby had a life-threatening illness. The treatment was going to be severe and painful. John would be literally taken to the brink of death by wiping out his entire immune system to prepare for the reintroduction of a donor's immune system. I was supposed to protect him from scary things and from getting hurt. It was my job as his mom to keep him safe from harm. Bumps and bruises would happen. A broken bone and stitches were part of most kids' childhoods. That was expected. But this? This wasn't supposed to happen. Kids shouldn't get this sick, especially contracting a disease that usually affects adults.

John's form of cancer—AML (acute myeloid leukemia)—was the form of leukemia that strikes adults. Children usually contract ALL (acute lymphocytic leukemia) and the cure rate for that form is much higher. Kids who contract AML need a bone marrow transplant. Chemo alone won't cure it. My children had appointments that week to have blood drawn to test for their compatibility as his donor. For the next several months, John's treatment would target killing the leukemia cells, as well as every blood cell in his bone marrow. The leukemia cells were called blasts. The reason John's shoulder had been so painful when he entered the hospital is because the blasts had multiplied in such a quantity that they were crowding the space in the bone and causing pain. Once the chemo does its thing, remission is achieved by obliterating all the blasts (or at least those that are visible through a microscope). Remission in AML only means that the blast cells cannot be seen in a section of the bone marrow that is extracted once chemo is done. Because the cancer begins in the marrow and runs through every blood vessel in the body, it is impossible to kill all the leukemia cells. Some are always hiding somewhere and will only continue to multiply. That is why a bone marrow transplant is the only cure. The donor's marrow takes over and creates healthy blood cells and transfers all its immunities to the patient. Whoever donated their marrow to John would give him all their immunities, allergies, and sensitivities. Once the chemo wiped out John's immune system in the marrow, his donor cells would be transplanted into him. It's a rather anticlimactic event. John would be prepared for the transplant with months of chemo and drugs to combat and prevent infections. Once his blood counts were at zero, the donor cells would be infused into his catheter just like a blood transfusion. John would need bags and bags of blood transfusions during the course of his treatment, both whole blood and platelets. Leukemia destroys these cells. When John was admitted, his CBC (complete blood count) was incredibly low. This is why he was so tired and bruised so easily. There were not enough red blood cells and platelets to keep him going.

There is a huge complication that can occur once the transplant is complete. Once the donor cells are grafted—they take hold in the marrow and multiply—the patient begins to feel better. His fatigue is lessened, he stops spontaneously bruising, and his color returns to normal. The hope is that the cells will continue to kill any stray leukemic cells, multiply, and take a firm hold in the marrow so that the graft becomes 100 percent of the patient's blood cells that were not ravaged by leukemia. The complication occurs when the patient's own body begins to reject the foreign bone marrow. It's the same principle as when a patient's body rejects a new transplanted heart, kidney, or other organ. It's just in reverse—the entire body rejects the new bone marrow. This is called graft-versus-host disease (GVHD), the graft being the new bone marrow and the host being the body. It is standard protocol to treat GVHD, as soon as symptoms begin to appear, with steroids. GVHD can be a fatal disease. It typically targets the skin, the gut, the liver, and the lungs. It is thought that GVHD should be prevented at all costs. It's a disease that can afflict the patient for years and end in death.

We had settled into the routine of our new normal hospital life. We brought up his favorite blanket and stuffed animals. We decorated his room with Britney Spears posters. His fifth-grade class made him a banner of a rainbow that said, "God keeps His promises," and it was signed by his teacher and all his classmates. We hung the banner right where John could see it. That banner came with us on every hospital admission for the next five years. John received his induction chemo for several days. He weathered the side effects quite well. With very effective antinausea drugs he was able to get through the treatment with minimal upset stomachs and vomiting. We called a friend who arranged for her hairdresser to visit John and give him a short haircut. It would be easier to manage once his hair started to fall out. Using a surgeon's cap during the loss of his hair kept it out of his face and off his pillow. We also had a professional photographer come in and take pictures of John while he still had his hair. We didn't have too many pictures of John. Our lives had gotten so crazy and busy that taking pictures of the kids had taken a back seat. I am grateful to have these pictures. John wore his favorite Orioles jersey. However, it is very apparent in these shots just how sick he was.

John was pretty much stuck in his room after the chemo. As the chemo worked, his blood cell count went down, and his immune system was not working the way it should. He was very susceptible to contracting infections from viruses, bacteria, and even the bacteria that normally lived in his own body. Visitors had to don gowns and masks to avoid transferring germs. Blood was taken every day from his port to grow cultures to check for infections and bacteria that could really make him sick. John watched a lot of TV! He was particularly happy to watch the cartoon cable channels the hospital TV had to offer. We did not have cable at home for our TV. We could only get a few of the network channels through our antenna. John also watched VHS movies on a cart that was wheeled into the room, and he went to the playroom to play games and work crafts. The child life specialist was a godsend! It was her job to make John's hospital experience less scary and as close to normal home life as possible. As John's blood counts continued to rise and he felt better, we were looking forward to going home. His blood counts needed to be at a certain level, and he needed to be free of fever before we could leave the hospital. We were counting the days.

Two weeks into our stay, John developed bad diarrhea. He had been complaining about his legs earlier in the day and had trouble walking. I had mentioned this to the doctor on call, but she didn't seem concerned. John's diarrhea continued for several hours. It had gotten so bad he was losing control and wasn't able to make it to the toilet in time. After cleaning him and the bed numerous times, I convinced him to wear a diaper to make things easier. He didn't seem to mind, which surprised me. He was ten years old and becoming very self-conscious about hygiene and his appearance. He even made a joke about it. At that time the show *Saturday Night Live* had featured a commercial spoof about adult diapers. The catch phrase the actors used each time they had an accident was "Oops, I crapped my pants." They uttered the line glibly and happily to get the message across that they were excited about using the product—which, of course, brings absolutely nobody joy. After changing John, the first time he had an accident using the diaper, he uttered, "Oops, I crapped my pants!" He cracked me up! But I worried that this new symptom was more serious than it appeared.

After getting John cleaned up for the umpteenth time, we settled in for the night. I noticed the nurses coming in more than usual to check his vitals. One would come in, then two would come in soon after. This happened for several hours. They didn't talk loudly, as they knew we were trying to sleep, but their urgent whispers sounded ominous. After several trips of medical personnel coming in to check John's monitors, a group of them walked in and turned on the light. I sat right up with a sick feeling: This wasn't good. They reported that John's blood pressure had been trending downward and was now at a somewhat dangerous level. They felt it was necessary to move him to the ICU for more intense monitoring. The ICU? What happened? Surely this wasn't because of the diarrhea. But then I remembered the trouble he had in his legs during the day and wondered if this was part of something more sinister. Several of them wheeled John and his bed out of the room and down the hall. I followed them, trying to keep it together so I wouldn't scare John, but I was terrified.

We arrived at the ICU, and they were putting him in one of the corner bays that was enclosed in glass. Because he was immune compromised, they needed to take extra precautions to keep him away from other patients and their families. I was asked to wait outside of the bay while the ICU nurses got him settled. He was hooked up to more monitors. I was told that Dr. Jeff, who lived in DC, was taking a wake-up shower and heading into the hospital. I noted that if his doctor was called and awakened at 2 a.m. and he was preparing to come in, this must be serious: more than the doc on call or interns were expected to handle. I eventually was allowed in, and I sat by his bed. I was so tired but couldn't sleep. An hour and a half later, Dr. Jeff arrived. He looked at me and I immediately knew this was a serious setback. I broke down in tears. He put his arm around me and said, "I know." I tearfully choked out that I didn't understand what was happening. We had only just begun to fight this insidious disease—how could it end so quickly? Always the optimist, Dr. Jeff said he was hoping that John had just "pooped himself out." That he had become severely dehydrated, which had caused his blood pressure to plummet. I had no idea if dehydration could do such damage, but it seemed like a plausible reason for this crisis, and I felt a tad better. He told me to go back to the room and try to sleep. He was there now and would watch John carefully, and we would have more answers in a few hours. If other serious symptoms appeared, he would come down and find me. I trudged back to the room, noticing the sympathetic glances from the nursing staff, and laid down. I never fell asleep. At 6 a.m. I called Jim and told him he needed to come up. I called Dot and told her what had happened, and I called my mom. She had not been able to visit us yet, as she had been fighting a bronchial infection for weeks and was afraid to be around John.

After my phone calls, I immediately went down to the ICU to check on him. He was hooked up to so many pumps! They had to put another access line in his wrist because the double lumen Hickman wasn't enough to handle all the drugs. His nurses were trying to get him to produce urine by giving him bags of saline. His kidneys were not operating as they should. His heart was not working normally either. After Jim arrived, the head doctor of the ICU ushered us into a room so they could try to explain what was happening to him. There we met the pediatric cardiologist, Dr. Love. Yes, a heart doctor was named Dr. Love! He told us that he believed that John's heart had been damaged by one of the chemo drugs he'd had. He called it cardiomyopathy, which is a diverse group of heart diseases that involve mechanical or electrical dysfunction of the heart. The heart does not pump blood correctly to all the parts of the body that need it. The heart is failing. He then proceeded to tell us that, in his experience and research, kids that suffer this type of failure either get better completely, get better somewhat and must rely on drugs and other therapies the rest of their lives, or die. He said John was very sick and that the next two or three days should be able to tell us in which direction he would go. Jim and I left that meeting in terror. I just couldn't wrap my head around the fact that my son, my baby, my child could die in the next twelve, twenty-four, or thirty-six hours.

Once the news traveled to our families and friends, a steady stream of visitors started coming up to the hospital. There could only be two people at a time in John's room, so those who really wanted to see him would visit with John for a few minutes. He was sedated and not able to talk or communicate with anyone. There was a small waiting room down the hall from the ICU and we camped out there for several days. Our loved ones brought us food, hugs, and company as we sat vigil waiting for news hopefully of John's improvement. That first day was a recurrent nightmare. Every so many hours, the staff would come down to find us if we weren't in his room to tell us of another organ failure and what they needed to do to keep him alive. One of those trips was to tell us that the damaged heart was allowing fluid to build up in his entire body and they needed to put him on several diuretics to drain the fluid off. The worst news was when they told us they needed to intubate him and put him on a ventilator because he was having trouble breathing on his own. I knew from talking to the team previously that day that once a patient is intubated it is sometimes very difficult to get them off it. I knew they had to do this to keep him alive and help him fight. After they intubated him, I went back into his room. I had never seen so many tubes, wires, pumps, and devices attached to a single human being. It just seemed hopeless to me at that moment. How could anyone survive after their body and organs had shut down to the extent that machines were doing all the work of living?

At times, I was distracted by the other families in the ICU with their desperately sick children. I could hear moms and dads speaking softly to their children, who were usually sedated, hoping that their words would comfort them and aid in their healing. I watched nervous dads pacing the floor and agonized moms silently crying as the doctor spoke to them. A few times I heard parents screaming and sobbing as their child succumbed to their illness or injury. Truly, this was the most terrifying and saddest place on earth.

I have vivid memories of praying the psalms by John's bedside. The ones that told God how desperate, abandoned, and bereft I felt. Where was He? How could He let a little innocent child like this suffer this extremely? How could He allow Jim and I to suffer this unspeakable reality? When I took a break and went down to the waiting room, my village was waiting to help me in whatever way they could. Mostly they just held me as I cried. I knelt on the floor and put my head on one of the chairs and sobbed.

At one point in the day, Dot, who was always present, took me aside and led me down to a small room. We were alone. She sat me down and looked deep into my eyes. As heartbroken as I was, I was still very aware of her horrible loss of her only daughter just months before. She asked me, "What are you most afraid of?" I looked at her like she was crazy. How could I possibly say out loud what my greatest fear was? It was too obscene, too huge, too horrifying to say. But again, she asked me: What was my greatest fear? I knew her well enough to know that she expected an answer. There was a lesson there. I choked out the words, "I am afraid my son will die." Then she quietly and gently said, "Yes, that is the worst thing that could happen." And now it is out there. Now it has lost some of its mystery. I have looked square at it by saying it out loud. And then Dot asked, "And what does your faith tell you?" I was in utter anguish, but I answered, "That God will take care of John and me no matter what happens." And she looked at me and hugged me. I knew in the depth of my soul that God was there, that He would carry me, and that no matter how this ended, He would lift me up and give me the strength, hope, and energy to journey through it. I had looked at the beast of my fear and I could no longer be paralyzed by it. John might die now. John might die later in the future. And if or when he does, I will somehow be OK.

CHAPTER 4:

Face Your Fears

——————

Fear is the most powerful of emotions. It prevents us from enjoying life, from loving ourselves, and from loving others. It stymies our potential and growth. We don't speak our truth because we are afraid of what others might think. We don't travel over bridges or fly in planes because we fear that they will crash or collapse. There are a lot of people in this country who are possibly realizing a new fear of going over bridges since the Key Bridge collapsed. Statistics are in our favor when they suggest that we will never be in a plane crash or on a bridge the moment it collapses—these are rare events. But this fear will prevent us from taking that trip to explore new places or spending time with our out-of-town loved ones. At its worst, fear can keep us from even leaving our homes. People suffering from agoraphobia can become prisoners in their own houses because they fear that something horrible will happen to them if they go outside.

Fear is paralyzing. Most times, fear doesn't make common sense. It is natural to fear getting a cold or virus, so we keep away temporarily from sick people. This makes practical sense, and it is smart to limit our exposure to germs, especially if we are immune compromised. But most fear is unsubstantiated or unfounded. There is no good reason for some of our fears. Some people fear snakes or spiders or mice. Chances are, a large percentage of these folks have never been bitten by a snake or a poisonous spider. Mice are a nuisance and can make a mess with their droppings, but they are tiny little rodents that are not known to hurt humans. Sure, these creatures may be ugly to look at but for the most part, lots of the snakes and spiders found in our homes or back-yards are harmless. But we fear them. We stand on chairs when we see a mouse as if they are going to attack us! If we took the time to remind ourselves that they are just as scared of us as we are of them and the odds are in our favor that they will not hurt us, perhaps we wouldn't have to feel so fearful. If we talked to someone we trusted or a therapist about our fear of going over bridges or of heights, we could very well dispel these fears and expand our experiences in life by doing these very things that frightened us before.

Without becoming too political, I believe the media is in the business of creating fear. They are constantly predicting doom and gloom and portraying every story in the worst possible light, because fear controls! We rarely see stories of good news. And news is reported not just as the facts of what happened, but we are bombarded all day long with how the reporters and anchors of whatever news channel you watch think about these stories. I believe the media is in the politicians' pockets and use the events of what's happening around us to conform to a particular politician's agenda. Living in fear is limiting at best and incapacitating at worst.

Facing my fear that my beautiful boy may die at only ten years old was terrifying but freeing. Being afraid of anything clouds the mind and controls our thoughts. Nurturing fear creates a downward spiral, and more fears take root. Before we know it, we are feeling depressed, and have a very difficult time looking at the bright side of anything! We begin to live in a state of hating to get out of bed in the morning, the heavy blanket of doom and gloom hugging us ever tighter. We begin to avoid our family and friends and ignore their loving attempts to contact us.

I have read many accounts of heroic people who were imprisoned and tortured, especially during WWII and Hitler's reign of terror against the Jewish people and others. Those who survived to tell the tale of their hideous experience possessed great faith in their God. They refused to let fear block out their faith. They nurtured and practiced their dependence on God every moment of every day. They lived through the gruesome quality of their existence only through persevering faith that God was taking care of them. I can't imagine anyone feeling more abandoned by

God than these people, and yet the survivors told tales of unspeakable, ghastly cruelty and how they endured it all through faith.

Facing my greatest fear that my baby could be taken from me was terrifying and gut-wrenching. Doing so, however, gave me the power to move forward to lovingly care for my son during whatever time we had left with him, and with God at my side I was filled with hope and strength.

The most common phrase in the Bible is "Fear not" or "Do not be afraid." Some researchers say it appears 365 times! Easy to say, of course, but not so easy to do. When we are faced with a scary ordeal or worrisome crisis, we tend to try to work it out by ourselves. We look for solutions and ways around it and attempt to control the situation with our limited knowledge or capability. However, so many problems fall beyond our control. There is nothing we can do to fix it. It is beyond our limited power to resolve. We allow ourselves to be consumed by worry and anxiety. We can't sleep. We can't eat, or we overeat. We can't concentrate on our work and are short tempered with those we love. We drink too much to numb out and not feel. However, if we have a relationship with God, why don't we trust Him with it? Why don't we take to heart the words He spoke so many times? He told us, "Fear not." He told us to trust Him. He told us to place all our worries with Him. He told us He would take care of us and give us all we need. Even if we do ask Him for help, many times we don't leave our trouble with Him. We take it back from Him and we hold onto the worry and anxiety, and suffer from the effects they create.

One of the most essential lessons I have learned is to give to God my worries and leave them with Him. Once I commend my troubles to Him, I am free from the debilitating effects of anxiety, fear, worry, apprehension, and unease. I live in complete trust that He will take care of it. I have had to acquiesce that I might not particularly care for the way He resolves my problem, but I trust that He knows what He is doing. I believe that He will work out the issue for my greatest benefit. Most times I don't understand why something played out the way it did, but if I gave it to God, then I trust it will be for my best interests in the long run.

My favorite verse in the Bible is Philippians 4:6–7: "Do not be anxious about anything, but in everything, by prayer and petition, with thanksgiving, present your requests to God. And the peace of God, which transcends all understanding, will guard your hearts and your minds, in Christ Jesus." Another is: "Fear is useless, what is needed is trust." Luke 8:50.

I honestly can't imagine any other way of living.

CHAPTER 5

He Belongs to You

JOHN SURVIVED THAT first day and night in the ICU. There were no concrete changes to indicate that he was getting better, but he was holding his own and the downward spiral of organ failure had slowed and appeared to have stopped. He was being supported by countless drugs, a ventilator that breathed for him, and a catheter to collect his urine. He was sedated so he could not suffer the pain or distress of being on the ventilator. He was bloated from the fluid that had collected all over his body because his heart was not functioning well enough to drain it off. He lay still, eyes closed, breathing tube snaking from his mouth, wearing only a diaper. The ventilator's breathing was the only sound. *Whoosh, click, whoosh, click, whoosh, click.* My eyes were glued to his monitors continuously displaying his heart rate, his blood pressure, his respirations, and other measurements I didn't understand. We were told all the normal ranges these numbers needed to be. When a value dipped, an alarm broke into the rhythmic pattern of the sound of the ventilator. If the value continued to stay low, nurses came in to adjust a pump or two, and silenced the alarm. My heart jumped every time an alarm sounded. I paced the room if it continued. If a nurse failed to show up to check it out, I went in search of them. I later realized that all monitors were replicated at the nursing station, and they could see everything that was happening. I learned to trust the purpose of the ICU—constant monitoring of severe and life-threatening illnesses. They were keenly aware of all that was going on with their patients, and their job was to keep them alive with all the power that modern medicine could give so that their bodies could heal.

Jim had gone home for the night, and I eventually went back to our hospital room alone. It was quite unusual for us to have access to John's hospital room while he was in the ICU. Their census was not high at that time, and they didn't need the room for another child yet. There was a common room next to the ICU where parents could rest or get a snack, and some parents slept on the padded benches. There was no other place to sleep, so if a parent wanted to stay at the hospital, that was their only option.

I walked into John's room and the stark reality hit me like a punch in the face that he wasn't there. A huge space was bare where his hospital bed once stood. He was down the hall fighting for his life. I picked up a blanket and spread it on the floor. I sat on it and the tears were streaming down my face. I had never felt such anguish. I felt helpless, knowing that this was something I could not fix or control. I was John's mom. I should be able to kiss away the boo-boo and stop him from hurting. I turned my thoughts to God. I was thinking about the time in Jesus' life when he was talking to the crowds and using the difficult language of being the "Bread of Life" and how He was food for them, and they should eat his body and drink his blood. Many of his followers walked away; they were frightened and confused by His words. Jesus had turned to his twelve apostles and asked them if they, too, would walk away. His disciples answered "Lord, to whom should we go? You have the words of everlasting life." These words had incredible meaning for me at this time. God was the only one I could turn to. He was the only one who could fix this. And so, I prayed. I told God how my heart was broken and that I had never experienced such excruciating sorrow. I told him how much I loved my son. I asked God to heal him. But then my prayer went in a totally unexpected direction. I thanked God for John and for allowing me to parent him for ten years. I acknowledged that John truly belonged to God: He was God's child first. The Lord had given me the joy and honor of raising him for ten years. The next words of my prayer truly surprised me. I told God that I would relinquish John back to him if that was God's plan. I gave John back to God! I asked for strength and comfort and lasting peace if the plan was for John to go back to God. I also explained to the Lord that I felt like I really wasn't finished raising John and I wanted more time with him. I didn't want him to die now and asked again if He could heal him.

After sitting on that thin hospital blanket on the floor for what seemed like hours, I got up, got ready for bed, and slept well for the first time since we had entered the hospital. John was in God's hands now and I gave up control. Whether John died or lived, I believed that God would take care of me and give me all I needed to weather the storm.

John stayed in the ICU for two weeks. He was gradually weaned from the ventilator and his numbers were trending in the right direction. His heart began to function normally and pumped the fluid off his body. He was in that one-third of kids who got better! He was finally discharged from the ICU and came back to his original hospital room. He had lost a lot of weight and was given a feeding tube down his throat into which high-caloric and vitamin-enriched formula was fed through into his stomach. He hated that so much. I can't imagine how uncomfortable it must have been to have a tube permanently in the back of your throat. His team started to talk about us going home!

Chapter 6

New Normal

AFTER SEVEN WEEKS in the hospital, John was finally cleared to go home. I had to learn how to flush his Hickman tubes and change the dressing over the wound every day. Flushing the tubes with saline solution and heparin was important to do so that the tubes remained clear and clean. John went home with a feeding tube, so I had to learn how to operate the pump that would deliver the formula to his tube. He also went home with TPN (total parenteral nutrition), another form of nutrition that was delivered through his Hickman. If we went out, he had to have a backpack to hold the bag of TPN, and a tube came from the pump into his Hickman. No one would ever know that he was being intravenously fed.

There were a lot of prescription meds I needed to fill for him. Swallowing pills was a stressful challenge for John. In the hospital the nurses and I had to beg, cajole, and bargain to get him to swallow pills. Many times, he gagged and threw up the meds, and we had to start over. He was only ten years old and up to this point all his children's meds had been in liquid form. I learned to crush up the pills and mix it with Jell-O. John took forever to eat Jell-O laced with his pills. I can imagine even Jell-O couldn't mask the bitter taste of them. One day John was trying to get down the drug-laced Jell-O and his older brothers walked in. They gently but comically made a little fun of poor John, that he had to have his pills smashed in food. From that day forward, John never ate Jell-O again. He swallowed all his pills. He got so good at it that when he was on about thirty medications, he could swallow an entire pile of them without a blink.

It wasn't long before I began to realize that our family was living our new normal. John had a regiment of medications and therapies. He wasn't allowed to eat seafood, milkshakes, raw vegetables including from salad bars, any fruit or vegetable that couldn't be washed, or any food that could harbor bacteria that his immune system couldn't fight. Everything had to be cooked. He had to wear a mask if we went out among a crowd of people, for example church or an inside activity like going to a movie theater or bowling lane. If he had a bad bout of diarrhea or vomiting or if his blood pressure spiked or if he started running a fever over 100.5 degrees or if he presented with pretty much any symptom that indicated that he could have an infection, we had to take him to the ER. We were instructed to call the clinic ahead and the ER staff would send us right up to the oncology floor where he would most likely be admitted. A fever is an indication of an infection and since John was immune compromised, he needed to be at the hospital, where they could treat him for what could be a fatal infection. Most of the infections would come from his own body and the normal bacteria that lived there. Many plans were interrupted because John would spike a fever and he had to go back to the hospital. This was particularly hard for us over the holidays and during family outings. Over the course of the next five years, John would be in the hospital at least once over Christmas, Easter, and Mother's Day and for some of the smaller holidays like Labor Day and Fourth of July. Many times, outings would be cut short and vacations interrupted if John spiked a fever. Because we lived only 7.3 miles from the hospital, and it took us only twenty minutes to get there, we were able to stay in our home. Many families who lived further away had to procure temporary housing in a Ronald McDonald House or other accommodations. The medical team told us that things could go south very quickly when a fever was present. A twenty-minute ride was the longest they felt comfortable with to get him to the ER for medical intervention.

I had been working for my Catholic parish full time when John got sick. I missed seven weeks when John was first diagnosed. After we got home from that first stay, I was able to return to work with the help of wonderful family members and friends who would stay with John at home so I could go to work. The church was only three blocks from our house, so I could come home in minutes if I needed to. My co-workers were kind and generous, taking on some of my work when I couldn't get to it. I asked my boss if I could be issued a laptop so I could still work when we were in the hospital. I went to work when John was home, and I worked from the hospital when John was there. If John was on a lengthy hospital stay of several weeks or months, I would stay at the hospital from Sunday night until Saturday night. I waited for Jim to arrive on Saturday evenings after he finished work and then I would leave and go home for approximately twenty-four hours. On Saturday nights I relished sleeping in my own bed with my five dogs. On Sundays I would attend mass and then come home and clean the entire house, sometimes doing bigger chores like washing windows or defrosting the freezer. Most people I suppose would have spent that time doing something for themselves or relaxing. Being a "doer" and a perfectionist, I needed to satisfy my need to make my surroundings better and cleaner. I liked to clean. It fulfilled my need to fix or make things the way I wanted. And most importantly, it gave me a sense of being in control. When I finished cleaning or organizing, I could stand back and see what I had accomplished, and I was in control of the situation. Nothing about John's illness was controllable. It was entirely out of my hands, and I couldn't make the cancer obey or conform. The house, the windows, the freezer, the laundry—now I could control that!

What I remember most from that time was how extremely exhausted I felt all the time. I was taking care of John, working at the church, trying to be there for my other kids, keeping up the laundry and cleaning. We were particularly blessed that our church family was sending us meals on an almost daily basis. Jim was working two jobs at that time. He had lost his job when Chrissy was going into high school. It took him six months to find another one, but it was only one-half of the pay of his original job. He took a second job in the evenings to supplement it. He was never home in the evenings when the kids came home from school, and none of them were very adept at cooking. The meals were a godsend!

I wish I could say that my kids perfectly stepped up to the task of taking care of themselves and the house. Katie was the youngest at thirteen and Chrissy was the oldest at nineteen. The boys were seventeen and fifteen. All of a sudden, their mom wasn't home for weeks at a time and Dad was always at work—six days a week, seventeen hours a day. And their baby brother was sick with a life-threatening disease. Their behavior reflected their risky and dangerous coping mechanisms. They drank alcohol—even Katie. They went to parties where there was lots of underage drinking. They came home very late, not respecting curfew, had friends over, and drank when I was at the hospital and Jim was at work. This was a time before cell phones. My friend Dot had gotten them each a pager so I could summon them when I needed them. This came in handy when John was in the ICU. However, I learned quickly that a pager is only a vehicle to let them know I wanted them to call. It didn't tell me where they were or if they were where they said they would be. There were a few calls in the middle of the night from the police and I had to pick them up from somewhere they shouldn't have been. I was certainly not a lackadaisical mom. I spoke to them often about the dangers of smoking, drinking, drinking while driving, and unprotected sex. I made it a point to get to know their friends and asked lots of questions about where they were going. I called parents to make sure alcohol wasn't being served at parties. I had to drive late at night to break up a party one of my sons attended at his girlfriend's house while her parents were out of town. There were a couple of DUIs issued and court appearances for underaged drinking citations. It was a challenging time to say the least. It almost seemed impossible to deal with. I was disappointed in them, feeling angry that their selfishness and reckless behavior was making my life so much harder than it already was. In hindsight I believe that their behaviors were not so different from others at their ages. They obviously didn't do these things alone. Their friends were all doing them too. They chose to cope with their world turning upside-down by partying and hanging out with friends—basic coping decisions by teenagers. Of course, I wished it had been different and they had behaved better and were a help to me with the house. I wished their choices hadn't caused me such grief on top of everything else I was dealing with. But that was our reality and later we realized we learned quite a bit from it.

Today my kids are amazing, hard-working, kind, and intelligent model citizens. Three of them are parents and I am very impressed with their parenting skills. I can count on each of them to be there for me and they are always in touch by phone or visits. I couldn't ask for better adult children who respect and care for their parents!

CHAPTER 7

Gritty Gratitude

DURING THIS TIME, more than at any other time in my life, I learned to cultivate an attitude of gratitude. I forced myself to look for each triumph, however small it was. There were a lot of difficulties and more trials than I had ever experienced. Every moment of every day was arduous. I had to push myself through overwhelming fatigue, fear about what was to come, mind-numbing thoughts about John's disease, and the effect it was having on him, me, and the entire family. I was consumed with worry over finances and how we could afford even the basic expenses of life.

Before John got sick, I worried a lot about money! The kids were often sick with viruses and infections, and trips to the pediatricians were almost weekly. Money was limited, as only Jim was working and I stayed home to take care of five kids. I complained constantly to anyone who would listen about how hard life was. I grumbled about how small our house was. I whined that my house was always a mess. I was a neat freak and liked things tidy, but with five kids, whose house wasn't a mess? It was like running against the wind. I bitched because Jim worked long hours and I had to deal with the house and kids by myself. I said things like "I hate my life" and "everything sucks." I guess I didn't expect things to be so burdensome and challenging. I was quite a miserable young woman. I became depressed easily. Each negative thought gave birth to another and soon my mood spiraled downward until I could find nothing good about my life. Boy, did I have a huge life lesson to learn in the future!

After John's diagnosis and during the years that followed, I began in earnest to "look at the bright side." Because it was such a trying time, it was next to impossible at first to find the bright spot and be grateful for it. Each time I discovered something for which to be grateful, I felt happy, even joy. I liked how it felt. I would continue to look for what was the impossible good that came from such a trying circumstance. I became grateful for days or weeks that we got to spend at home where we could sleep in our own beds, not being interrupted every couple of hours by nurses coming in to take vitals or draw blood. That tiny house that was too small suddenly became my respite and my sanctuary. I cherished each day and night I could spend there. I was grateful that cooked meals kept coming even when we were home, so I didn't have to cook—I hated cooking! I was grateful that I could clean my house and "control" something. I needed to feel satisfied about an accomplishment I had achieved. If that was a clean house or shining-clear windows or a defrosted freezer, then so be it. It was enough. I never dreamed that the "ordinary" could become so life-giving and sought after.

I was eternally grateful for my many friends and family members who walked with us. I could never thank them enough, especially my friends Dot, Mary, Diana, and Rita and my sister Patty and sisters-in-law Barb, Sherri, and Betty, and my mom. They cooked for me, and they stayed with John at home and at the hospital so I could go to work or to a doctor's appointment. They tried to "ride herd" on my teenagers, checking up on them frequently. They gave them rides to high school events and took them shopping for things they needed. They took John on special outings so I could go to work or have a day to myself.

During the years that John battled his disease, we would receive many, many cards and get-well wishes and gifts of money. Our finances were stretched to the limit, and many times I thought we would have to declare bankruptcy. Our debts to the hospital and personal debts continued to grow. I was only being paid when I could work. We did have medical insurance, but it only covered so much. There were thousands of dollars of out-of-pocket expenses for which we were responsible. I was immensely grateful for all those who gave so generously their treasure so we could keep our heads above water.

I believe that God puts people in your life when you will especially need them. Dot had an amazing relationship with John, and he looked to her to talk about things he couldn't with me. As he grew into a teenager, he had many questions about his body and his feelings. She was the youth minister at our church and worked with teens. She was invaluable to me and to John as she patiently and lovingly listened and counseled John about his thoughts and emotions, especially during those eight months he knew the unimaginable truth that he was going to die. It was not lost on me that as I had comforted her when her only daughter was killed in a car accident, here she was doing the same for me. Dot and I were very different. She was worldly, having lived in many different places. She was a lot of fun and had so much wisdom about many things. I admired her for her absolute honesty and the confidence she exuded. She loved fiercely and completely. I was quieter and more sheltered. I hadn't really been out of my hometown for decades. I had only traveled with my parents when I was a kid, and have never been out of the country. I didn't know anything about teenagers and at one time I had four of them! I was shy and hesitated to speak my truth in front of others. I was not confident in myself and felt inadequate. She helped me enormously in finding myself, and I learned from her to speak up and advocate not just for John but for myself! I often told her I should pay her in addition to paying my therapist. Most of the things I learned about myself in therapy were the same bits of wisdom she had shared with me in previous conversations.

Mary was my forever friend I had met in my junior year of high school. She saved me from being friendless and her love aided in my healing from the bullying I had suffered. We spoke on the phone every day while our children were growing up, sharing the joys and trials of raising children. When John got sick, she brought me the most amazing chicken salad sandwiches when we were in the hospital. She would show up at my house with a dozen casseroles I could freeze and serve later, and her signature homemade cheesecakes! She didn't much like pets, and I knew her love for me was the real thing when she came to my house with our five dogs to care for John so I could go to work. One day, one of the dogs brought in a dead squirrel and laid it at her feet.

Not only did she have to dispose of the squirrel but clean up the dog's vomit, as she had eaten most of it. Now, that was a real friend!

I met Rita in the first year of John's treatment at the University of Maryland hospital. Her husband Dave and their daughter Katie were in the playroom of the oncology floor when John and I came in one day. Katie was in treatment for ALL (acute lymphoblastic leukemia). We had a wonderful chat, and John and Katie also hit it off. Rita and Dave would take turns staying at the hospital with Katie. They also had a little boy, Chris. Dave told me when Rita was going to be with Katie and the next day, I searched the rooms until I found her. We became instant friends! We had so much in common, but at the forefront was that both our kids were fighting leukemia. We could identify with each other's feelings of frustration, exhaustion, and fear. We would notify each other when we were headed to the hospital. When Katie was admitted I would visit her and Rita, and when John was admitted, Rita would visit us. We would hide wine-coolers in our underwear in our luggage. After 9/11 our luggage was searched each time we came in, so we had to be creative in how we disguised it. When our children were asleep, we would come to one of our rooms and enjoy an "adult beverage." Rita would bring in a small refrigerator when she came so our drinks would be cold. We used red Solo cups, so no one knew that we were drinking! We would spend summer days at Dave and Rita's house, where we enjoyed their in-ground pool. We celebrated New Year's Eve together and our families enjoyed summer camp for sick kids at the same time.

I met Diana when Chrissy was in the first grade. Her daughter Maria was in Chrissy's class, and they became friends. Diana is my spiritual sister. She is intelligent and sensitive and always searching for the truth about herself and God. She fearlessly delved into the mysteries of life and God and was eager to share with me the truth she had discovered, and I was just as eager to learn from her. She taught me to expand my mind and to not just accept things at face value. There were hidden meanings in everything if we took the time to look for them. Because I was a rule follower, I was hesitant to peek around what I was taught, to bend the rule enough to look behind it and find the reason it was made.

She helped me to discover my courage to question and explore what I couldn't make sense of and accept that either it would remain a mystery to me, or I would replace my ideas with thoughts that satisfied my new understanding.

I was grateful for John's hero-like team of doctors, nurses, PAs, fellows, interns, etc., who cared for him during his long illness. These people became part of our family. We shared much more than John's disease and medical treatment. They would celebrate with us some of life's greatest milestones—our twenty-fifth wedding anniversary and kids' graduations. They would go out of their way to bring John some food that he wanted, or stay late if we needed to talk. We were friends sharing life in this most unconventional way. I knew that during their medical training they had been advised against getting too close to patients and their families. But as one of them said to me, there are those families that are just impossible not to fall in love with. During John's last years, we celebrated his birthday at Hooters in the city. Some of his team would come by after their shifts and celebrate with us. I am grateful for Dr. Allen, Dr. Jeff, Diane, Chrissy, Tessa, and Dawn from the University of Maryland; and Dr. Allen, Dr. Meghan, Nancy, Lisa, Colleen, Dr. Kristin, Dr. Heather, Kim, Kelly, Ron and Melissa from Johns Hopkins; as well as many, many more whose names I don't remember but were just as important to us. I am still in touch with some of them to this day.

I was grateful for the faculty and administration at both of John's schools—St. Clare Elementary and Middle School and Archbishop Curley High School. His teachers constantly assisted him in his studies so that he would not fall too far behind. They were patient with deadlines for papers and homework, knowing he was not feeling well a good part of the time. Carlien and Judy, two of his middle school teachers, tutored him after school. They gave up their free time to teach him and help him to learn. For John to attend his sophomore year at Curley, we had to ask for special accommodations. He was then in a wheelchair because the long-term steroid drugs he was on had damaged his long bones in his legs and created stress fractures in his vertebrae in his back, which made it painful for him to walk. He was also on oxygen because he was having breathing issues due to a suspected infiltration from graft-versus-host disease (GVHD). The school did not have an elevator for its three floors, and we didn't know how John would be able to attend with these special needs. We met with the administration and were assured that they would welcome him back and make it completely possible for him to get to his classes safely. At the beginning of the school year, they asked the football team members to assist John in getting to his classes. A group of them volunteered to learn his schedule and meet him after every class to take him to his next class. If his class was on another floor, the guys would just pick him up in his chair and carry him down the stairs. These guys—Steve, Bo, Billy, Kevin, and Rob—will always have a special place in my heart. John wanted most of all to be normal—to attend school every day, to work on his studies, to enjoy high school life the best he could. He did not want to stay in bed and play endless video games to pass the time. He wanted to experience life! These young men granted John his greatest wish in life—to just blend in and be one of the guys. I learned that these guys and indeed many of the young men that attended Curley while John was there were truly inspired by John's courage and heroic persistence to live life to the fullest, even if it was just going to school every day.

Thanking God for each blessing, both large and small, became a habit. I intentionally looked for the silver lining in each trial. I thanked God for each benefit I enjoyed, fully aware that there are people who don't have these advantages. I thanked God for my comfy bed at night and roof over my head, knowing that there are many, even in my own community, who sleep in the woods on newspapers or old blankets. I thanked God that I could work. I've had jobs I loved and those I hated. But I was able to make a living that provided my family with what they needed. I thanked God for my health. Even though John was struggling, I was healthy enough to take care of him, to provide for him and enjoy him. I thanked God for dirty dishes and stinky laundry because I knew I had food to eat and clothes to wear. I thanked God for my car so I could get John to the hospital. Many families I had met during John's treatment had to take a city bus.

Pretty soon I realized I was grateful in all situations, good and bad. I was grateful if I got a good parking spot in the hospital garage because I was close to the elevator and wouldn't have to push John's wheelchair too far. And I was grateful if we ended up in a parking spot that was furthest from the elevator because that would mean I would be forced to walk farther, and I needed the exercise! I was grateful for the days or weeks we could stay at home. I was grateful for the time we had to stay in the hospital, because that meant John was still with us. I forced myself to be grateful for everything—good things that made my life easier and bad things that made my life harder—because I knew I would learn something important amid hardship. I thanked God for sunny days and rainy days, both having their own merit. I thanked God when I had energy and I thanked God when I was exhausted, because I knew at the end of a day I could sleep, at home or at the hospital. Both beds gave me restorative sleep, whether in my own comfy bed or the chair-turned-into-a-bed at the hospital. I would bring an extra foam pad and my own blankets to the hospital, so it had a little bit of a home atmosphere.

I didn't know it at the time, but the carefully cultivated attitude of gratitude in all things would become another lifeline to which I would cling. There would be very painful times ahead for my family, and I know I couldn't have navigated them with hope without my armor of gratitude. Life is indeed a war, with many small skirmishes and large battles. Every instance when I thanked God for anything, I was given ammunition to fight the enemy of negativity. Negative thoughts kill lifegiving concepts of hope, trust, and joy. Negativity breeds negativity. Negative thoughts multiply at an alarming rate until we become despondent and fall into despair. It's a terrible place to be. I recently heard the phrase, "You live most of your life in your mind. Make it a happy place to be." You have the power and courage and perseverance to create a grateful heart and positive mind. God gave these virtues to you when He created you. You have a choice every day to be gloomy or happy. It's up to you. Your circumstances in your life don't rule your mind. The trials, difficulties, and pain that you might encounter each day do not have to control your thoughts unless you let them. Being grateful in the gritty, grimy, deepest, darkest, and scariest moments in your life will change you, and you will have achieved every person's common goal—how to be happy and joyful in all circumstances!

Chapter 8:

The Cure

JOHN SURVIVED HIS induction chemo and heart failure in the ICU. He would have to come back to the hospital three more times to receive maintenance chemo to keep him in remission. Leukemic cells would continue to multiply because they were part of his immune system in his bone marrow. Chemo would kill the bulk of these cells, but a bone marrow transplant would be the only treatment that could cure him. Chemo is toxic. It has to be to destroy stubborn leukemic cells. Chemo also kills the good cells needed to keep your body alive and make life-essential red and white blood cells and platelets. There is a reason there is a skull and crossbones on each bag of chemo. It's essentially poison and gives the patient horrible side effects. John suffered all of them—losing all the hair on his body, including eyebrows, lashes, and body hair. He was nauseated often and vomited a lot. He lost weight. He had fevers from his body giving in to bacterial infections because his immune system would be essentially wiped out during each chemo session. Each chemo regimen required about a two- to three-week hospital stay. They would administer the chemo according to protocol— usually several days of infusions. Then we would wait until his blood counts dipped very, very low and watched for fevers. After they hit the lowest point necessary to maintain remission, they would gradually rebound and come back up. Once John's blood counts were at a specific level, he would be released, and we would come home. If he spiked a fever or had any troubling symptoms, we would return to the hospital for antibiotic infusions. Every couple of days we would go to the day clinic where John would get infusions of red blood cells or platelets because leukemic cells destroyed these cells. I learned very quickly how essential it was for people to donate blood. John would not have survived without these donated blood cells. After four months of these cycles of chemo and restoration of blood cells, a date was set for his bone marrow transplant—the only known cure for AML. All four of his siblings were tested to see if any of them could be a donor. They tested six variables in each child's blood. Chrissy was a six out of six match! She would be his donor and hopefully save his life!

Chrissy was the best possible choice for many reasons. She was the oldest and possessed the maturity to understand the gravity of her gift of her bone marrow. She wasn't afraid of needles or necessary medical procedures, and we all believed she could handle the stress of the donation better than her siblings. John's doctors took her aside and explained the procedure. She would be sedated, and a large needle would be inserted into her hips to harvest her life-saving bone marrow. She would not feel anything during the procedure but would be sore afterwards and would need some pain medicine. The doctor also told her that, even though she was the perfect match, she was still respected for the unique person she was and did not have to do this. She told us later that she felt she absolutely had to do this whether she wanted to or not. She was her brother's only shot at life and she wouldn't be able to live with herself if she didn't do it. One of the most important pieces of information she received that day was not what she or any of us expected. She was told that she should not feel guilty if this transplant didn't work and John's leukemia returned. It would not be her fault in any way. I know the doctor felt it was important to tell her this, but he might as well have talked to the chair. Chrissy would carry this fake sense of guilt for almost two decades later. No one could convince her otherwise, and how utterly unfair it was that she suffered immense conflict and sadness that almost killed her seventeen years later.

John and I checked into the University of Maryland Hospital on a hot day in June to ready him for his transplant. John would be infused with a concoction of extremely strong and powerful chemo. The goal was to wipe out his immune system entirely. Everything had to go—

every blood cell that could be seen through a microscope. His blood counts would go to zero, nada, nothing. A big fat goose egg would be written on his white erase board to signal that his body was ready for the transplant. It had been decided to not give him the same drug that had possibly caused his cardiomyopathy during his induction chemo, so they substituted another one instead. They had also decided not to subject him to total body radiation, which was standard protocol. This was radiation that would target every part of his body, ensuring that all blood cells in his marrow would be annihilated. The date for his transplant would be finalized when his blood count was at zero.

The numerous side effects and possible complications were explained to us in alarming detail. This would be no walk in the park. John could suffer even more unpleasant and painful effects from this chemo. In addition to the nausea and vomiting, he would develop sores throughout his mouth and throat. The chemo was so powerful that the quick-growing cells in his mouth could not rejuvenate fast enough because there was toxicity in his system preventing them from growing. There were other complications that could occur, but I only remember the ones John lived through. We were also told that this treatment was possibly fatal. The patient could develop a life-threatening infection his body wouldn't be able to fight. They would use big-guns antibiotics to combat the infection but sometimes it just wouldn't work. We were introduced to the disease of graft-versus-host. John's body could reject his donated marrow and cause all kinds of complications and he could lose his life. Jim and I were terrified. If John was scared, he didn't let on. He just wanted to get it over with so he could go back to his ordinary life.

The transplant would take place in one of the ICU rooms that had walls and a door. John would need to be isolated for a few weeks until his immune system bounced back. There was another boy who was receiving his transplant in June and had already started his treatment. He had a large hospital room with an entire bed for the accompanying parent. It was spacious and much more pleasant than the small ICU room. The University of Maryland Hospital had only been doing bone marrow transplants for a year or so and only had one "transplant" room.

The day came for the transplant, and Jim brought Chrissy to the hospital. Her procedure was done in the morning. I was able to pop over to see her several times while she was in the recovery room. She was doing well, and comfortable with pain meds onboard. It was much later before John received her donation. Her donation of marrow was treated for several things to make it even more compatible for John. They eventually brought in the bag of her donation. It looked like a bag of blood but larger. They hooked it up to John's Hickman and let it infuse. The doctor stayed in the room with us to watch for any initial adverse reactions while Chrissy's marrow was introduced into John's body. It was rather anticlimactic to say the least. It was really nothing more than a blood or platelet transfusion that John had previously received dozens of times. But this was the cure! This would make him cancer free!

The infusion ran its course, and it was done. I took Chrissy home to recover for the weekend, and Jim stayed with John. Chrissy was very, very sore and it took several days for her to be pain free. John was confined to the ICU room, where he watched TV and played video games. He was in good spirits.

Maybe two or three weeks into our stay, we got word that we were moving into the transplant room where the other boy had been. I learned sadly that he had passed away during his treatment. I saw his mom crying and I hugged her. There were no words. I was heartbroken for her and terrified for me, wondering if that was John's fate as well. We moved into the transplant room, where John experienced the worst of his post-chemo symptoms. He lost even more weight, as he couldn't keep any food or drink down. He suffered terribly from sores in his mouth and throat. He was miserable and slept most of the time. He didn't, however, seem to display any signs of GVHD, which was good. One night I heard a loud crash and realized that one of his nurses had dropped a bottle of IVIG—donated blood product to assist in rebuilding his immune system. It was in a glass bottle and the pieces went everywhere! I then heard a very small weak voice asking his nurse, "Are you OK?" Here my sweet son was concerned about whether his nurse got hurt, and he was suffering so terribly.

John's eleventh birthday was coming up while he was in isolation in the ICU. We asked him if he wanted anything special. He decided that he wanted every person who came into his room to wear a hat. Any kind of hat. The funnier the better. Everyone who came in had to wear a gown and facemask after washing their hands vigorously in hospital antibiotic soap. Sure enough, every medical personnel and visitor who came to see him that day wore a hat. The ICU staff had disseminated the information that it was John's birthday and he wanted everyone to wear a hat. Crazy Hat Day was a success! And it pleased John to no end that everyone thought enough of him to abide by his wishes, even if they were a little crazy!

John's immune system slowly started to revive, and his mouth and throat sores began to heal. He still couldn't keep any food down and was being fed through TPN. As each day brought news of regenerated cells, the plan to go home was being discussed. John had to demonstrate that he could eat, or he would have to have a feeding tube again. His memories of his feeding tube from March spurred him on to begin to try to eat and focus on keeping it down. He would try to eat just one cracker and would promptly throw it up. In a few hours he would try again. We started to think that maybe it was mind over matter and that, because he had been vomiting for so many weeks, in his mind the logical conclusion was that he would vomit everything he ate. We suggested he play a video game and while he was concentrating on the game, he could mindlessly eat a cracker. After several tries, it finally worked and he was on his way to tackling this problem, bringing him closer to going home.

Finally, we were released from the hospital and began to settle down at home. We made some minor improvements in the house that included getting cable set up for the TV. John could finally watch the TV programs he had enjoyed in the hospital and those his friends were watching. The older kids were thrilled that our family had come out of the stone age and had access to the TV programming that all their friends had had for years. We got John some new video games and movies to watch. He learned to be content with these forms of entertainment, as he was unable to play sports with his friends. John would not be able to return to school for another nine months. We contracted with a tutor from Baltimore County who would come to the house and teach him what he should have been learning in the sixth grade. John worked hard at his studies and excelled, yearning for the day when he could return to school and his friends.

CHAPTER 9

Hope Does Not Disappoint

THE DEFINITION OF HOPE in the Oxford Dictionary is: "A feeling of expectation and desire for a certain thing to happen or a desire accompanied with expectation of or belief in fulfillment." We use this term frequently in our lives. We hope we pass the test. We hope we get the job. We hope we can find the perfect dress for our wedding. But if these things don't happen, we realize there will be another chance to pass the test, another job to apply for, and other dresses in other shops we can look at. Not really a big deal if these things don't come to pass. We get over our disappointment and try again. Then there's the more serious desires. I hope she gets better from this illness. I hope they don't get into an accident driving during a snowstorm. I hope he doesn't die during the risky surgery. I hope I will get pregnant this time after suffering so many failed attempts. If these things don't happen the way I had hoped, it is a much bigger disappointment and often the beginning of a very difficult and sorrowful time in our lives.

To me, hope means more about what God wants for me than my own desires. I can tell God what I hope for. *I hope that John gets better. I hope the bone marrow transplant works and cures his leukemia. I hope our life gets back to normal and we can be free from hospital admissions and treatments.* Of course I wanted all these things. I wanted them more than I desired anything else. Ultimately, though, I was beginning to realize that hope meant more about trusting that God was in charge and knew the big picture. He knew me more than I knew myself and He knew what I needed and what was best for me. I believed He didn't make bad things happen—He didn't cause John to get ill. It happened because the world is fallen and imperfect, and people have free will to choose between good and evil. I do believe that God can and does intervene and prevent bad things from happening when He chooses. I do not believe that His intervention is random or capricious. God has a plan for every one of us and He allows things to happen or not happen, depending on His plan and what He needs us to learn. And of course, we have the free will to either try to learn from a difficult event or not.

In the Bible, Romans 5:5 states: "And hope does not disappoint, because the love of God has been poured out within our hearts through the Holy Spirit who was given to us." It took me a very long time to understand this. My immediate thought was, "Of course, hope can disappoint. I don't get a lot of things I hope for." It was only by living through these darkest of days that I gained understanding. Hope can never disappoint if God is holding you. He is Hope. We cling to Him with the deep knowledge that He will take care of us. No matter how this event or crisis is resolved, we will be fine. We might be sad and plunged into agonizing grief, but He will be carrying us through it. We never have to fear that we won't attain what we hope for. God will always give us the very best. We can't understand how or why He works something out in a certain way. But we don't need to understand. Someone once told me that it is wise to learn to become comfortable with the mystery. We humans in the twenty-first century want to know everything! We want to know how things work and why bad things happen so we can prevent them. We don't like it when something doesn't make sense to us. This searching for answers is mostly a good thing. Seeking resolutions to problems is what makes us evolve and create ways to make life more trouble-free for everyone. I am quite relieved that I live in this century with all its medical advancements, appliances to make me physically comfortable, and tools to make my household jobs easier. With summer approaching, I am most grateful to Willis Carrier, who invented the air-conditioner. But many times, there just aren't any answers to our questions. We will most probably never know the answer to life's most stubborn mysteries, and we need to accept that. We humbly place our questions before God and trust in hope that He is working it all out for the best.

CHAPTER 10:

The Fail

LIFE RETURNED TO AS NORMAL as it was going to be for now. John had medicine to take and many trips to the clinic to check on his progress in rebuilding his immune system. He returned to school in April 2001 and was excited to be among his friends again. He had kept up his studies and comfortably fit back into place in his classes.

As spring bloomed around us and John was feeling well, I felt my body and mind relax, feeling joyful that hopefully this nightmare was behind us. I loved springtime. The trees and scrubs coming to life again and flowers popping up everywhere with their vibrant colors and pleasing fragrances. I hoped with every fiber of my being that new life in spring would also mean new life for John. The docs had assured me that John's marrow was showing 100 percent of the graft, meaning Chrissy's marrow had completely taken over in John's bones. He now had Chrissy's immune system. All her allergies would be his. All her immunities would be his.

He would need to be inoculated with vaccines again, but for now Chrissy's immune system would do the work. In the back of my mind, I knew that cancer returned in many patients and that people fell out of remission. I wanted to believe that he was totally cured, never having to face this disease again. But I was also a very practical person, and the fear of it returning never quite left my mind.

In May we were due in for a clinic visit. I was surprised that I was feeling a little unsettled. I thought I was probably imagining things, but I had noticed in the last few weeks that John was sporting some new bruises and his gums bled when he brushed his teeth. He seemed fine but I knew in my gut that something wasn't right. When we arrived at the clinic, John had his usual blood draw, temperature, and blood pressure taken and answered lots of questions about how he was feeling. I took the doc aside and told her I had a gut feeling that something wasn't right. I expressed my fear that the cancer had returned. The doc brushed my concerns aside and told me that John was fine and to stop worrying. I had told Diane, head nurse at the clinic, of my concerns. She had been with us from the beginning. She said he is probably fine, but she would call me in the morning if something was wrong.

When the phone rang the next morning and I could see that it was University of Maryland, my heart stopped. Diane said she would call me if anything was wrong. When I answered, Diane said to me, "You are right, something is going on." We took John the next day for a bone marrow biopsy that would tell us if the leukemia had returned. We waited in the familiar chairs while John was taken to the procedure room for another aspiration of his hip bone. He had been through several of these aspirations and had asked that he be truly sedated with the "white stuff," or propofol (the drug Michael Jackson used as a sleeping aid and fatally overdosed on). He enjoyed counting backwards when the anesthesiologist administered the drug to see how far he could get. It was a game for him to see if he could count higher each time. When the doc entered the waiting area after they finished John's aspiration, they asked us to come into the "doom and gloom" room. I already knew what they were going to say, and it wasn't good news. Unfortunately, John is out of remission, they said. His marrow was showing leukemia blasts again. The transplant hadn't worked. We were told that we would be referred to Johns Hopkins Hospital, since the University of Maryland was not equipped to handle more serious cases of returning leukemia, particularly AML. We left the room in silence and joined John in the recovery room, where we gently told him the news. He cried. I cried. The nurses cried. We all were forced back into the reality that treatment would have to begin again; that pain and suffering would take a front seat in John's life again. Again, I would have to watch my baby being tortured with needles and biopsies and painful procedures and having to endure the unpleasant and agonizing side effects of nausea, vomiting, mouth and throat sores, fevers, and infections. I could hardly bear the thought of it all. It was unimaginable to think that John had to go through this torment again and to imagine the stress that would be put on our family.

The day we found out John had relapsed was Chrissy's birthday. We came home from the clinic, and the entire family went out to dinner to celebrate Chrissy's birthday. Chrissy was trying to process the fact that we would probably need to ask her to donate her marrow again. After dinner while driving home, we passed the community's funeral home. John, very nonchalantly, pointed at it and told us that was the funeral home he wanted us to use when he died. Jim and I were stunned and tried our best to hold back the tears. This eleven-year-old was wise beyond his years and the bravest boy I knew.

Our parish was holding their annual carnival. It was the highlight event of the year and all the kids from the school couldn't wait to ride the amusements, eat hot dogs and fried dough, and hopefully win a prize at the stands. John and his friends were old enough to hang out in groups on their own without adults, and John couldn't wait to be there.

We had a meeting with Dr. Allen at Hopkins that first day of the carnival. We drove to Hopkins and navigated the parking lot and huge hospital until we found the pediatric oncology clinic. The floor was much larger than the pediatric floor at the University of Maryland. There was a large waiting room separated by a door that went to the clinic side and then again to the inpatient side. We were soon ushered into a clinic exam room, and met with Dr. Allen. It was spacious and bright with large windows to let the sunshine in, and happy murals and paintings hung on the wall. Dr. Allen asked John how he was feeling, and John shyly answered, "OK." Dr. Allen then got right to it. He said that John's relapse of AML put him in a higher risk of care. We basically had three options:

1. We could treat him with another marrow transplant using Chrissy's cells. He would undergo total body radiation this time and be infused with different and somewhat more powerful chemo drugs. His marrow would not be treated as extensively as the first time,

which would allow GVHD to develop. He then explained that, although protocol for a first transplant is to treat the patient so that he doesn't develop GVHD, the thinking is different for a second transplant. Since GVHD is the host (patient) attacking or rejecting the graft (marrow), it is hoped that if allowed to develop and spread to an extent, this process would also attack and kill any leukemia cells still lurking in the patient's body. John's disease is obviously very stubborn and came back in only nine months or even sooner since we don't know when the cells started to grow again.

2. This option would be to force GVHD to develop in John's body without a bone marrow transplant, but the severity of the GVHD would be great and there was a higher chance of deadly and fatal complications.

3. Do nothing. Apparently, both above options were so dangerous and life threatening, sometimes the better option would be to not put the patient through it, as it was likely he would die anyway. Doing nothing would mean waiting for the leukemia to grow and eventually kill him. He would of course be given lots of support to keep him comfortable. But my baby would die in the next few months to weeks.

I tried to wrap my head around the severity of the situation. It seemed hopeless that my son would survive his cancer. I looked at John. He was silently crying and looking out the window, not wanting us to see his tears. Of course, he had heard all of it. How can a boy so young process the possibility of his impending death? I know I wasn't ready to throw in the towel. I said to Dr. Allen that we weren't ready to call it quits and asked him which, besides the "do nothing" option, was the best one of the two remaining treatment plans. He answered that he thought another bone marrow transplant would give John the greatest odds of staying alive. We looked at John and asked him if he was OK with doing another transplant. He just shook his head in agreement, and we asked Dr. Allen what the next steps were.

Dr. Allen asked if John had his "Make a Wish" wish yet. I told him that we had a trip scheduled in June to take a Disney Cruise. He said that we had to move fast and get John into induction chemo again in a week's time. He told us that we needed to try to reschedule and take that trip now. I just looked at him, not able to process what he had just said and the full meaning behind it. He again reiterated that we needed to take the trip now and leave, like, tomorrow! He then gently said that John would most likely be too sick for a long time to be well enough to take a trip anytime in the future. He didn't have to say it, but I knew he also meant that John might die and never take the trip.

We left Hopkins in a daze. I just couldn't wrap my head around the last few days. It had all happened so fast. Even though I carried around a worrisome suspicion that John had relapsed, not until I heard the words did it really sink in. It was a gut punch, and we were still living in the nightmare. We took John to the carnival, and he immediately found his friends and was having fun for hours. I found Dot, who over-saw one of the game stands for the Youth Ministry group. She took one look at my face and took me away from the merriment of the carnival and into her office. There, the flood of tears gushed forth again. I was between shock and agony. I couldn't believe it was happening again and I knew what misery John and our family would experience again.

CHAPTER 11

Courage Is Not the Absence of Fear

COURAGE DOES NOT MEAN that you are not afraid. To have courage is to face whatever it is that scares you. Courage is what makes a firefighter run towards a burning house. You can't tell me that he is not afraid of the danger of the smoke and flames. He must certainly have a healthy fear of dangerous situations. But he trusts himself and maybe a Higher Power that, using his training and skills, he can push through the danger and save a person's life. Courage is what makes a person tell the truth about himself, someone else, or a situation, even if he is afraid of what the person hearing it will think about him or say to him. Whistle-blowers display courage when they report an unsafe practice at their company, knowing that they could lose their jobs in the process. Courage is that virtue that gives you the power to stare down your fears and learn truths you may think you aren't ready to know. But knowing truths, especially about yourself, can only bring you to a better understanding about yourself and closer to that person you were created to be.

So many people have remarked through the years on John's courage. He was just a little boy, and he was facing a big adult problem. Any child with cancer must be courageous. But John wasn't brave just because he had cancer. Having cancer did not somehow automatically give him courage. It was the way he handled his disease and lived his life despite his cancer. He was remarkable in the fact that he didn't complain and managed to maintain a positive and cheerful attitude most of the time. He would share with me and especially with Dot his frustrations and grief about what he had lost—his health, his innocence, some friends, his athletic ability, and just being a normal kid. Yes, he cried in pain and whimpered when he vomited for the twentieth time a day, but I never heard him say anything nasty to his medical team, to our friends and family members who helped to care for him, or to anyone. John looked at his disease squarely in the eyes and vowed to do all that his medical team asked him to do to fight it. Every time there was a new procedure or treatment for the many complications that threatened his body, John accepted it and went through with it. I remember one time he wanted to go camping with the Boy Scouts and it was several months post-transplant. The doctors said he had to wear a mask because the mold spores in the forest bed could be a danger to him, causing a fungal infection. I knew he didn't want to wear it. He was in his early teens by then and very self-conscious about his body and how he looked. He wanted to just be a normal boy scout and not be singled out as the "sick kid." I told him he should wear it, reminding him how awful it was to have a fungal infection and how nasty the medicine was that he would have to take. The medicine (amphotericin) that was used to treat fungal infections was nicknamed "amphoterrible" by the nurses because of its nasty side effects. I figured he wouldn't wear it and I had to let it slide. He needed some control over his disease. I later found out he had worn it. He hated it but wore it anyway, being courageous enough to do what he deemed was right for him despite what the other kids might say. I never heard if anyone made fun of him. John probably wouldn't have told me anyway.

John displayed courage during his high school orientation. It was supposed to be an overnight, retreat-like experience that gave the new freshmen an overview of their new school and the meaning of the brotherhood of Curley men. Because John was experiencing chronic diarrhea and bone pain from his GVHD, he decided he didn't want to spend the night there and use the locker room bathrooms and sleep on the floor. So I dropped him off and picked him up in the evening for the two days. It was in August, and it was hot! He told me after the first day that he had been tempted to do something that was wrong but didn't. Apparently, the soda machine was broken, and kids were able to open the doors and take out sodas without paying for them. Lots of boys were taking advantage of the open machine and took sodas. John said he was thirsty. He was always thirsty due to some of the meds he was taking, and he carried a huge water bottle around with him. He was coaxed by several boys to just take a soda since he was so thirsty. John knew that it was virtually stealing and refused. He wanted a soda but didn't take it. Some of the kids called him a coward but he stood his ground. He was courageous.

Courage is a gift from God. We can all have it. We just need to ask. Maybe we don't want courage because it means we might have to face something scary and deal with it. Most times we don't have a choice about encountering scary things in life. They happen to everyone. Bad things happen all the time. We can hide when they do and wait it out until it's over, but then we miss out on witnessing and experiencing the most powerful and inspiring truths and wisdom that a human being is capable of grasping.

John wrote these words for his Curley Yearbook the year before he died:

Courage does not mean just one thing. It is more than just being brave. It is being able to accept and overcome the hardships that life gives you, even though you are afraid or just want to give up. As some of you might know, I have been living with cancer for four years now. I have had to accept that I have this disease, fight to stay alive and overcome the fear of being different. I also had to accept the fact that there were things I couldn't do anymore. When I was younger, I was very athletic and loved to play sports. Knowing that I am limited in my physical activity, it takes courage to accept my loss and explore other ways to use my talents. Because I missed a lot of school, I had to work hard to make up work and keep my grades up. I missed my friends and social activities. It took courage not to give up when it seemed that so much was taken away from me. Courage is also demonstrated at

Curley. The students show courage when they help me with my books or climbing the stairs, not being afraid of what someone else might say. Courage is demonstrated when someone comes to sit next to me at lunch and they don't even know me. Courage is shown every time a Curley student does what is right, even though they might be ridiculed. Anyone can have courage. God is always with you, especially in the hard times. Knowing this, you never have to be afraid.

CHAPTER 12

Second Chance and Acute GVHD

WE MET WITH DR. ALLEN at Hopkins on a Wednesday. The next day, Thursday, I spent much of the day on the phone trying to reschedule our Make a Wish trip to Disney ASAP. The cruise would not be available to us on such short notice, so we opted to spend a week at Disney World. We would stay at a resort in nearby Kissimmee, Florida, called "Give Kids the World." It would serve as our accommodations for the week, offering meals, entertainment, and a spacious condo. There were goodies and trinkets left in our condo every day for the family, free meals at their dining hall, free ice cream any time of day or night, carousel rides, pool privileges, and shows. We had a rented van to go back and forth to the Disney parks. Make a Wish Foundation funded the entire trip, including airfare, limo ride to the airport, accommodations, rental van, and even spending cash for souvenirs and anything special we might want.

When I got home from work on Thursday, after telling my boss I would be taking a week-long trip, I frantically started packing. We were leaving the very next morning! I realized we didn't have any luggage. Our family had never taken a trip or flown before. We spent a week every summer at Ocean City but most of our belongings were packed in boxes or bags. My dear friend Diana went out and bought us a complete set of luggage, enough suitcases for each of our kids and Jim and me! Her generosity knew no bounds! My sister-in-law Barb took my daughters out to get new bathing suits. It was May and they had not had the opportunity to get new ones for this summer. Of course, their old ones from last summer would not fit, or so they said!

My mind was racing. How would I ever begin to get everything ready in time to fly out the next morning? I was excited for this gift of family time and fun, but also knew that our urgency in leaving so quickly meant that John was in another race for his life. Somehow, I managed to get it all together. The kids who were in college and high school were able to take their midterms on Thursday, and some of their teachers waived the requirement altogether. Friday morning, a limo arrived to take us to the airport and our adventure began!

The vacation was wonderful! Give Kids the World was an extraordinary place that catered to sick children and their families. Every need and want was met with kindness, compassion, and love. John received a button that identified him as staying in Give Kids the World, and we were able to go to the head of every line of every attraction at the Disney parks. We laughed together and played together and absolutely enjoyed one another. Joe was our resident comedian and kept us laughing all week. We relaxed at the pool and enjoyed the thrills of the rides. It was perfect and bittersweet. As delightful as the vacation was for us, we were reminded every day that this was John's Wish. This was the one thing he wanted to get to do with his family because he had a serious, life-threatening disease. He might not have another chance to experience the magnificent opportunity to have this much fun in the happiest place in the world, because he might die. Sometimes I would look at him when he wasn't aware and I could see the dread and apprehension on his face, undoubtedly thinking about what was coming.

He would be admitted back to University of Maryland for his induction chemo the day after we came home. After that, he would go to Hopkins for his second bone marrow transplant in a year. I am comforted so often by the sweet memories made on that trip and am forever grateful for all those who contributed to Make a Wish and Give Kids the World to make it possible.

John's induction chemo at University of Maryland went smoothly and although he suffered the usual dreadful side effects, the hospital stay was pretty much uneventful for him. This time, however, turned out to be a milestone for me, although probably not the best or healthiest. It was the first time in my life that I had ever gotten drunk! I did not drink during my teen years and mildly used alcohol during my early years of marriage. I had never drunk enough alcohol to erase my inhibitions and buzz me sufficiently that I was numb to the current surroundings and circumstances. I had decided long ago that I didn't want to feel out of control and avoided anything that could make me feel that way.

We had an older station wagon at that time. One Saturday Barb was staying with John at the hospital for the day while Jim and I had something else we needed to do. I was driving Jim up to the hospital for his usual stayover on Saturday night and noticed that the car was overheating. I was able to get it to the drop-off spot at the hospital and parked. Steam was pouring out of the hood. I got out of the car and opened the hood to allow the steam to escape. I knew enough not to open the radiator but apparently the poor hospital parking attendant did not. Before I could shout "NO!" he had put his hand on the radiator cap and turned it. An explosion of extremely hot water and antifreeze drenched him and fell on me. He immediately ran into the hospital for medical assistance. I fortunately did not get any of the molten liquid on my skin, only my clothes. At that moment, I felt utterly defeated. John was fighting for his life—AGAIN. Our life was turned upside down AGAIN. Instead of catching up with our finances and becoming solvent, we were heading deeper into debt AGAIN. And now the stupid car that we relied on so much had failed us AGAIN.

Jim went into the hospital to relieve Barb and I called for a tow truck. I also called Dot and asked her to come and pick me and Barb up. After sitting on the curb for literally hours, the tow truck arrived, and Dot and her daughter's best friend Melissa, Barb, and I headed home. No one had eaten dinner yet and it was late in the evening, so we decided to stop at TGIF for dinner. Chrissy was working there as a hostess and seated us. I firmly believe that a conspiracy was created by my companions that I needed a nice, big buzz. And for the first time in my life, I allowed it to happen. I drank several Ultimate (huge) daiquiris and then a couple of shots. In the end I didn't become fall-down sloppy drunk, but I felt fun and giddy and laughed at everything. It was a euphoric feeling, and I wasn't focusing on my troubles at all. We all enjoyed an entertaining ride home as I was told that I was funny! Dot put me to bed, making sure I had lots of water and an aspirin, and I was no worse for wear in the morning. I certainly did not make a habit of this and yes, there were years ahead in which I purposely drank to try to feel better. As you will read later in this book, both my daughters became addicts of alcohol and drugs, and I learned fast that depending on mind-altering substances was a terrible way to live.

John's second bone marrow transplant went off without a hitch. He endured the usual nausea and vomiting and mouth sores. He would be playing one of his video games, pause the game to vomit, and go right back to it, never missing a beat. He seemed to take it all in stride, which made me feel a little relieved. I loathed having to watch him suffer. Chrissy donated her marrow via pheresis instead of an aspiration under sedation. This was much easier on her, as she only had to undergo needles in both her arms much like a blood donation. Her blood was drawn from her body in one arm, spun through a machine that filtered out the cells needed for the marrow, and put back into her body through her other arm. Her friend Maria stayed with her the entire time, keeping her company. Once her donation was ready, it was transfused into John the same way as the first time, and he didn't have any serious reactions.

Now the watch was on for signs of GVHD. Everything about this transplant was calculated to ensure that GVHD would develop to have the antileukemia effect. There are two kinds of GVHD—acute and chronic. Acute GVHD would occur within the first hundred days after transplant and could affect the skin, GI tract, and liver. Chronic GVHD would occur either during that time but in most cases approximately two years following transplant and affect the skin, mouth, liver, lungs, GI tract, muscles, joints, and genitals. The docs were pretty confident that John would develop acute GVHD because they didn't take any precautions against it.

John certainly did develop acute GVHD and suffered skin, gastrointestinal, and liver involvement. The docs monitored him closely so that as soon as they observed that his liver involvement was getting close to dangerous, they would administer steroids to halt the process. The problem was that they really didn't know when enough was enough. How much GVHD involvement would keep the leukemic cells from reforming? How long did John need to suffer with GVHD to avoid a relapse? There was not enough data for them to know for certain what that sweet spot was. John's liver enzymes were carefully observed and when the values got dangerously critical, they reined GVHD in by giving him steroids. His agonizing symptoms gradually abated, and he began to feel well again.

He was in the hospital for this second transplant for about two months. I remember it well because one of those days was September 11, 2001. Barb called me that morning and told me to put the TV on. I was supposed to go to work that day, and Rita was coming up to stay with John. I remember driving to the church and hearing in real time when the World Trade Center buildings collapsed. I got to the church in time to see all the kids at the school being unofficially dismissed as their parents just came to the school and demanded that their kids be released. I decided to drive right back to the hospital. If the world was going to end, I wanted to be with John, and Rita should be with her family. I spent the rest of those weeks glued to the TV (when John would let me). He did not want to see any of that horror—I guess because he was living his own.

Eventually John got over his acute GVHD and he was discharged to go home. Post-transplant life began again, and the hope was tenuously optimistic that this would finally be the end of his disease.

CHAPTER 13:

Is It Really That Important?

ONE OF THE GREATEST lessons I learned from John's long illness was captured in a popular book written by Richard Carlson: *Don't Sweat the Small Stuff*. After months and years of coping with a child with cancer, the truth in this book became my own. All the stuff I used to worry about and lose sleep over became trivial and of absolutely no importance to me. Because I was a type-A perfectionist, I wanted everything to be done my way. The house needed to be cleaned to my standards. Everything in my house needed to be organized to my specifications, including closets, drawers, and laundry. We always needed to be on time for everything. We had to accept every invitation to outings, parties, and gatherings. I worried about things I said to others, often feeling foolish or afraid that it probably sounded stupid. I felt quite self-righteous and judged others if they didn't share my value system. I wanted to be right in every discussion, and I dismissed others' opinions if they didn't mirror mine. I would harbor resentment and hurt feelings for a long time if I was hurt by someone. Everything that wasn't the way I wanted it to be became a battle. "Choose your battles" wasn't even in my thought process. I didn't know how to relax, and every day was spent "doing." I identified myself by what I could accomplish. I was the sum of my "doing." I didn't know how to just be.

Because I was forced to navigate one of the most difficult roads in life, I learned that most of what I had deemed important just wasn't. It really didn't matter if my house was clean, my laundry properly folded, or my closets organized. I was just too tired to care and didn't have the energy to get this stuff done. I really could live among the chaos and be at peace. It wasn't important anymore if we went to every function we were invited to. If we couldn't attend, I would make my apologies and the hosts would have to understand. And if they didn't, well, so what? I found out rather quickly who my true friends were in life and who weren't. Most importantly, I learned to speak up. I especially learned to speak up and become an advocate for John during his treatment. On one occasion in particular, my mama-bear protection characteristic exploded. John had been admitted for GVHD complications and was going to try a new experimental trial for skin involvement. It had been a trying day, as he was uncomfortable and absolutely did not want to be there, and I was exhausted. At five minutes to five in the afternoon, a doc entered our room and said he was going to do a punch biopsy on John's rash. The team was usually very good about explaining all the procedures and tests John would need for any of his treatment, but I had not been informed of this biopsy. I did not want John to endure any more pain that day, especially if I didn't know the reason for it. I told the doc that he couldn't do the punch and had to wait until I talked to the team. The doc was obviously irritated by my refusal, and looked at his watch and said, "Look, I need to get this done now. I get off work at 5." I looked at him and firmly told him that he did not have my consent. I then marched out of the room and went over to the clinic to find one of John's team. When I found Dr. Allen, I told him that I didn't know that a biopsy was needed and didn't want to consent until I knew why John needed it. Dr. Allen told me that in order for John to be accepted into the medical trial, he would have to have some tests, including a skin biopsy, to be considered a candidate. This was all news to me! I was just told that he was admitted to try a new drug. Dr. Allen apologized that the team had unfortunately not informed me of everything about the trial, and I went back to John's room. The biopsy was scheduled for the next day, and I was given lots of information to read about the trial.

I learned to share my thoughts and feelings with others and was comfortable with it. I no longer worried about what they thought of what I said. I became more confident in accepting that I was entitled to speak my truth the same as everyone else. If someone didn't like me for my truth, it was OK. I didn't need them. I knew who my faithful village of friends was. If someone hurt my feelings by something they said to or about me, I let it go. How they felt about me was none of my business. No longer did my self-worth plummet from an insensitive or cruel comment. I did not give others the power to change how I valued myself.

I realized that all the silly stuff that had crowded my mind was keeping me from discovering the true joys of life, like relationships with those I loved. After John got sick, we spent more time enjoying each other as a family. Because of the generosity of foundations like Casey Cares and Believe in Tomorrow, we could enjoy outings together that we could not have afforded otherwise. We ate dinner together most nights and watched TV and laughed a lot. I have known many people who haven't talked to a sibling or friend for years because of some stupid argument they had a long time ago. Please, let that stuff go! There is no time for that! Life is short and unpredictable. At any moment it can change, and you can lose the opportunity to speak to a loved one ever again. Don't hold onto grudges and resentments. Deal with them now and mend bridges. Nothing is as important or life-giving or forever as love. When you die, let love be the only thing you take with you. It is the only thing that truly endures.

CHAPTER 14

Chronic GVHD

A FTER JOHN RETURNED HOME from his second transplant, life returned to post-transplant existence. John would return to the clinic several times a week for check-ups. We were vigilant for signs of fevers or infections. John had tutors at home until he returned to school in the seventh grade.

Those years were marked with lots of hospital admissions. He had gastrointestinal infections like C-diff, lots of fevers of unknown origin (they never figured out why he had a fever), and fungal infections (including one in his lung, which caused him to have a lung biopsy and be kept in the hospital over Christmas). He had renal complications and was monitored by a cardiologist because of his cardiomyopathy during induction chemo in 2000. He suffered a grand mal seizure at a youth ministry meeting one evening and was admitted for two weeks for tests to see why. They never found the cause and he never had another one.

On one Mother's Day during this time, John was feeling fine all day. We went to my mom's house for a spaghetti dinner. Suddenly John spiked a fever and started vomiting. I called the emergency line at the clinic and told them we were coming in. The doc on call didn't think it was an emergency and told us we could wait it out. He was new and didn't know John. I told him that I suspected that this was serious, and we were bringing him in. When we arrived, John was immediately put in a room and hooked up to monitors. Not long after, as I watched the monitors, John's blood pressure started trending down. I alerted the medical team, and a host of doctors and nurses came in. They said they had to move him into a bigger exam room. I sat in a chair a few feet away as a crowd of doctors worked on John. My eyes glued to the monitors, I realized that he was in trouble. His blood pressure was so low. They put a tube in his nose to drain his stomach contents and hooked him up to several IV pumps delivering meds. They told me he had sepsis, an infection in the blood stream that can lead to organ failure and is often fatal. As soon as he was stable enough, he was transferred to the ICU. He was somewhat conscious and was complaining about the tube in his nose. He also expressed his fear that he would need a ventilator. I tried to console him the best I could and let the team work on him. The next day I had a coffee with Kristin, one of his doctors, in the cafeteria. She said this was serious and he could die. But knowing John, we hoped that he would pull through. I spent the nights in a room set aside for parents who had kids in the ICU. There were several beds, each surrounded by curtains to maintain a level of privacy. There was also a bathroom where we could take a shower. I spent the days at John's bedside and took a few breaks in between in the area where the elevators were. Once I fell asleep on the chairs, vaguely aware of the constant ding of the elevators. I was so tired I could sleep anywhere. I was numb with fear that this time John would succumb to his disease, but he surprised us all. He eventually began to heal, and we were discharged to a regular room.

If John wasn't in the hospital he would be at school or visiting with his friends. He was in his teen years by then and became interested in girls. He still loved video games and horror movies. Unfortunately, most of his friends had drifted away and didn't invite him to outings or visit him. I suspect because John didn't have the energy or stamina to play sports or outside games and tired easily, they lost interest or just didn't know how to relate to him. John had written in his journal for several months how unbearably lonely he was. However, his two best friends, Brent and Keith, stayed by his side. They were his ride-or-die buddies. They visited John at home often. John was a guest at their houses for sleepovers and outings. They kept him in the loop of what they were doing or into. They came with us on vacations to the beach. One or both were always around. And I was so incredibly grateful for them! I remember I was bullied as a young teen and had no real friends. I couldn't bear to see John suffer from this same unbearable loneliness.

John desperately wanted to play sports again. One summer, a community football league in our area was forming. John wanted to go out for it. I was terrified. Football was dangerous and he could get hurt. I told him he absolutely couldn't do it. John responded that he would ask Dr. Allen at his next clinic appointment. And that was exactly what he did. I was shocked to the core at his answer. I looked at Dr. Allen in stunned silence as he told John that yes, he could play football. He could do anything he felt he was capable of doing. If looks could kill, Dr. Allen would have been dead. I didn't want John to do anything that could hurt him. He had been hurt enough from the disease. After wrestling with myself for a couple of days, I acquiesced and allowed John to play. I really didn't want John to hold back on anything he wanted to do. I didn't want him to be defined by his disease and I begrudgingly knew Dr. Allen was right. I drove him to registration, secretly hoping John would change his mind. He didn't, and it was time for the first practice. I had talked to the coaches about what John had been through and assured them his doctor had given him the "go ahead" to play. John did OK and the next weekend there was a game. I saw that most of the kids on his and the opposing team were bigger than John. Everything in me wanted to pull John out of the game but I spent the next agonizing hour peeking out from under my hat at the match, my eyes peeled on John when he was played. He wasn't on the field very much, for which I was grateful, and finally it was over. The next practice was on a very hot day. I dropped John off at the field and went home. I received a phone call from one of the coaches saying that I should pick John up. When I got to the field, John was waiting for me, extremely out of breath and red in the face. I didn't say anything and took him home. Sometime later, John admitted he really wasn't up to the physical exertion needed to even run, and he reluctantly told me that he didn't want to play. I felt so bad for him. This was another loss among many that he had to accept. Even though I was terrified for him I really wanted him to succeed at something he really liked. I realized it was important for him to come to this decision for himself. He had no regrets; at least he tried.

John was acutely aware that he was a teenager, but his body was not reflecting the changes he yearned for. He still had the body of a child, did not grow pubic hair, didn't have a need for deodorant, which is one of the first signs a boy is growing into a man, and didn't have any changes to his genitals. At about fifteen years of age, John talked to his medical team about it. It was suggested that he could wear a testosterone patch that would force his body into puberty. John was elated! He called it his "sex" patch. Soon he was experiencing those most sought-after changes. He didn't want to talk to me about it (moms are not usually privy to such intimate conversations with their sons) but he did call Dot every time he experienced a new sign that he was becoming a man. I cannot thank her enough for being that person that John could confide his deepest desires to, and his medical team for responding so pastorally to something that was of utmost significance to John.

John developed suspicious rashes and frequent uncontrolled diarrhea. Each time I noticed a new rash or bump, we would go to the clinic. Most of those times he was admitted for biopsies of the skin and his gut through a colonoscopy. One such time he was scheduled for a colonoscopy. There is significant preparation that must be endured before this test can be performed. He was not allowed to eat anything solid the day before and had to succumb to the enema prep to clean out his bowels from any stool. The next morning, as we waited for transport to take him to the test, we got word that it had been delayed. Just another couple of hours, we were told. John was hungry and whined a little about not being able to eat. For the next eight hours we waited for him to go for the test. Finally, at a little after 5 p.m., we were told that the staff was quitting for the day, and it had been rescheduled for the next day. And they said that John still could not eat anything until the test was over tomorrow. I heard my newfound voice tell them, "No, sorry, John will eat. It's not his fault that you couldn't manage your schedule better. You will have to deal with it." I then ordered John some food.

Hospital time is different than any other time anywhere! Tests being delayed happened frequently. Thankfully most of them didn't require John to fast from eating. The worst was when we were waiting to be discharged. If we were told it would happen in the morning, we would be discharged in the afternoon. If we were told it would be in the afternoon, it would be dark and nighttime before we left. We learned to get used to it and made a lot of tongue-in-cheek jokes about it. We learned to adapt. If we had somewhere we needed to go in the evening, we realized we may or may not be able to go. John learned too to go with the flow, although I know he was disappointed many times. He spent so much of his time in the hospital. When they said he could go home, he just wanted to go!

After several biopsies, the docs really didn't achieve any clinical evidence that he had chronic GVHD but because he had so many of the symptoms, they were going to treat him for it. And that meant more steroids! He was also put in a clinical trial for new drugs and had a treatment called photopheresis that was found to be effective in treating GVHD involvement of the skin. John would undergo basically what Chrissy had to do to harvest her blood. But his treatment would expose his blood to ultraviolet light to damage and kill off some of the donor cells that were causing the GVHD. Funny that a transplant's purpose was to give the recipient the cells of someone else and now we were trying to kill them. Even just remembering it now reminds me of just how delicate a balance this all was, and how much of the treatment was a lot of educated guesswork and assumptions. John began this treatment, and we met Tom, the technician who would run the procedure and take care of John during it. Each treatment took several hours to complete. John brought in DVDs to watch, much to Tom's delight! Many times, there weren't any other patients there and John got lost in his shows, and Tom and I talked about anything and everything. John did not have a Hickman catheter any longer so he had a fistula put in his thigh, which was a vessel under the skin that the needles would access. John's veins were in bad shape and, since this treatment involved so many sticks, the fistula was a godsend. After several treatments John's rash cleared up nicely and this procedure was deemed successful, ensuring that John would continue with them for the foreseeable future.

We were thrilled that the photopheresis was working on John's skin rashes, but it didn't seem to alleviate John's diarrhea. He dealt with that unpleasant symptom for the rest of his life. At home it wasn't so much of an issue. John had become at least tolerant of my cleaning him up from an accident, even though he was a teen. The diarrhea became a huge problem for him when he went out. He was embarrassed in store restrooms and other public places when he couldn't get to the toilet in time. One time we had to buy him new underwear and shorts in the store for him to wear out of the bathroom. We learned then to bring extra clothing for him when we went out.

John attended "cancer camp," or Camp Sunrise, every year in August. It was a camp run by Hopkins staff for chronically or seriously ill kids in their care. He loved it and met some of his dearest friends there, including Jarrett and Elizabeth.

He was quite fond of Elizabeth and wrote about his feelings for her in his journal. He yearned to have a girlfriend! All his buddies had entered the world of girls and dating, and he desired more than anything to live the normal life of a teen boy and fall in love. One year, on our wedding anniversary, we picked up Elizabeth and took her and John to the Candlelight Inn, where we all had dinner, but at separate tables at opposite ends of the restaurant. John asked Elizabeth to his homecoming dance at Curley and that beautiful, sweet girl accepted. John was attached to portable oxygen and hung back against the wall, feeling embarrassed by his medical equipment. Elizabeth grabbed his hand and pulled him onto the dance floor and started dancing wildly. He had no choice but to join in and it became one of his most heartwarming memories. These two events became the only "dating" John would ever experience.

Attending camp was not only a wonderful and fun week for him, but it also gave me some much-needed time off from his care. One year the diarrhea was especially bad. He tried to deal with it the best he could but was trapped in a restroom for hours because he had had an accident and didn't have any clean clothes with him. Thankfully, one of the staff noticed he wasn't there for some activity and went in search of him. It truly broke my heart to know that he suffered for who knows how long in humiliation because of his unreliable body. Another time, John wanted to sleep out in the tents with the other kids. He toughed it out for a few hours, but unfortunately had to ask to go back to the infirmary to finish the night because he couldn't breathe well without his oxygen. John handled these betrayals from his body with grace.

I'm sure he was frustrated and angry that he couldn't enjoy camp like everyone else, but he never showed it.

John also attended special camps, Camp Fantastic in Virginia and Camp Sunshine in Maine for kids with life-threatening diseases and their families. He cherished these experiences and I have saved his souvenirs and crafts he accumulated from his times at camp.

Because of the long-term steroid protocol, John began to suffer pain in his legs and back. He had the steroid "bloat," gaining weight in his face and belly, was always thirsty and hungry, and had trouble sleeping and relaxing. He had x-rays of his legs and back that showed stress fractures in his vertebrae and bone damage in his long bones in his legs. There really wasn't much they could do for him for his back, as fractures were found in most of his spine, but there was a procedure that could possibly relieve the pain in his legs and knees. We were referred to Sinai Hospital and an orthopedic surgeon explained that he would drill small holes in his bones connected to his knees, and this would tease the bone to regrow and cover the areas that were literally eaten away by the steroids. John had this outpatient surgery and in time he did experience relief from this pain.

After several years of dealing with chronic GVHD John was taking approximately thirty different drugs. He was on prophylactic drugs to keep him from getting bacterial infections and ones to avoid fungal infections. Steroids are amazingly effective for many issues, but they weaken your immune system, so John was still very much immune compromised. He was on drugs to support his heart and his kidneys and to prevent seizures (since he had had one). He took pills to control his blood pressure (several hospital admissions for that issue) and pills to regulate his triglycerides. The fat in his blood was so thick that it floated to the top of the test tube like fat in gravy. He had narcotics he could take for pain and for anxiety. He had some nasty liquid medicine that could only be obtained from one pharmacy to help his diarrhea. I don't know what was worse—having to drink the foul-tasting med or having diarrhea. At some point his blood sugar was out of control and he needed insulin injections. One time when John was admitted to the hospital for some kind of infection, I remember the resident doc on call admitted to me that John was the most complicated kid they had on service. I didn't know if I should be afraid of that designation or be thankful that he was still alive! Our out-of-pocket expense for John's drugs alone was $800 a month. But they kept him going and he desperately wanted to keep living.

John's graduation from the eighth grade was a momentous occasion! He had been in and out of school for long periods of time since the fifth grade. He worked hard at his studies with his tutors when he couldn't attend school, and with the help of Carlien and Judy, his middle school teachers at St. Clare who tutored him after school, he accomplished all the requirements of his curriculum to graduate with his class. When his name was called to receive his diploma, his entire class stood up and clapped and cheered for him, bringing the entire congregation to their feet! The standing ovation lasted for several minutes. I sobbed happy tears as I was overcome with admiration for him and the love I felt from my spectacular village. On a somewhat funny note, poor Bryan Warner received his diploma right after John. His mom, Mary, who was a good friend of mine, jokingly remarked that Bryan had to follow a tough act!

Summer 2004 brought the promise of a relaxing summer filled with happy trips to the beach and fun times with friends. We did those things and more, and I was in awe that my boy was still with us and valiantly coping with his chronic disease. The good news was that he remained in remission. No leukemia cells evident! But GVHD was hanging on with a vengeance with no end in sight. John agreed to all the treatments that were available to combat the effects of this disease, and was a warrior in its management. We were told that eventually the disease would "burn itself out," but it was unknown how long that could be. In the meantime, we went along with the status quo and lived life.

CHAPTER 15

John's Decision

IN AUGUST I RECEIVED a call from Hopkins that someone who owned a beach house on Fenwick Island wanted to give a family a week at the beach. Kim, our child life specialist, immediately thought of us and asked if we would like to accept the generosity of this person and use their house for a week. Of course, I said YES! Jim couldn't go, as it was next to impossible for him to take a week off from the post office on such short notice. The other kids were working or back at college, so it was just John and me. I asked my sister Patty if she wanted to join us with her two kids, John and Carly, and my mom. They all happily agreed, and we headed to the beach. We had a wonderful time! The house was a block from the ocean and was stunning! I have many great pictures from our week, and I am comforted by the warm memories.

There was only one dark spot, however, that caused me to worry. Even though the house was a short walk to the ocean, John had a difficult time walking there. His breathing was often labored, and he was out of breath when we got there. This was a new development. He had had breathing problems in the past post-transplant and especially when he had had a fungal infection in his lungs. He had had to be supported with oxygen before but always healed enough to get off it. I was especially concerned because I knew GVHD could affect the lungs. It attacked the lungs in a way that made them irreversibly fibrotic. It created scarring that made the lungs stiff, and it would be harder to breathe. There was no cure for this type of GVHD involvement and no reversal. Once the lungs became fibrotic, they stayed that way. This type of GVHD was usually fatal. I tried to keep my fears at bay, and made a mental note to call the clinic on the Monday we returned home.

Once we were home, I made the call, and we went to the clinic. They listened to John's lungs and set up a series of tests that were not invasive but would measure his lung capacity. Unfortunately, his test results were poor, and we were referred to a pulmonologist. Since John's lung capacity was severely diminished, they advised against a lung biopsy that could tell them more about what was going on. In other words, they deemed him too sick to be able to survive this procedure without the help of a ventilator. And John flat-out refused anything that might mean he had to go back on that machine. John was placed on oxygen. We were given an oxygen converter machine for home that turned the room air into oxygen. This eliminated the use of bulky, heavy oxygen tanks. We were given, however, some smaller tanks to use when we left the house. The machine made a constantly whirring noise while it was operating, which was twenty-four hours a day. John had tubing that allowed him to go anywhere on the first floor of the house. We got used to stepping over tubing and avoided tripping. John also received a wheelchair, since he got winded so quickly while walking.

John's sophomore year was starting soon, and we had our meeting with Curley's administration. The plan was made, and beginning day one the volunteer football players took him to his classes. We made sure he had several oxygen tanks placed in the guidance office. If he was getting low, he would go there, and the staff of the office was trained to change out the tanks. For the first couple months of fall, he insisted on going to school every day. He did his homework and assignments and studied for tests. He didn't want any special treatment. He wanted to be treated just like the other students—no extended deadlines, no shortened assignments, and no extra allowances. More than ever, he wanted to be in control of his life and do it on his own.

In November, around Thanksgiving, John decided he wanted to have a meeting with his entire hospital team—his docs, PAs, nurses, child life specialist, everyone! He wanted to know what his prognosis was going forward. Those sweet, caring people decided on a time, and they all assembled in an exam room in the clinic. John presided over the "meeting" and asked outright what his future looked like. Dr. Allen said that they suspected GVHD involvement of his lungs, based on his symptoms. They couldn't be sure without a lung biopsy, and they felt John was too sick to survive that. If he did, he would probably be on a ventilator and might not come off it. He continued that there was one treatment they could try, but it had never been done. It was based on a theory or hunch only. They would deliver one of the chemo drugs he had been on previously and they hoped it would halt the GVHD progression so that it didn't continue to destroy his lungs. He wouldn't get any better and was stuck with the damage he had already suffered, but the expectation was that the GVHD would be stopped in its tracks and not create any more damage. He would never have the health he had before leukemia and would depend on oxygen the rest of his life, but he could possibly live a long time. The risk of this treatment, other than the obvious (that it had never been done, so side effects and complications were unknown), was that John's lungs might not be able to handle the toxin and he would have to be put on a ventilator. John asked again about the statistics on this treatment. Dr. Allen reminded him that it had never been done. There were no statistics. No data. No reassurance that this would or could work. John fell silent for a moment. He asked if that was it. Was there nothing else they could do? Everyone just looked at him sadly. John didn't hesitate with what he had to say next. He wanted to go home. He wanted no more treatment. He wanted to live his life the best way he could, knowing he would die sometime in the near future. He asked how much time he had left. He was told there was no way to tell. I found out later that Hopkins made it a point not to put a time limit on time left. They believed that a patient's will was so strong that many of them lived far longer than what the medical team suspected. John thanked everyone, and most of them quietly left the room. Kim, Nancy, and Colleen stayed back and talked to Jim, John, and me about palliative care, hospice, and what John's life would be like now. I learned much later how much the team admired our courage in allowing John to make his own choice. John was fifteen. He was a minor and we were responsible for his care. We could have demanded he take the last-ditch option. In fact, Colleen told us that 99 percent of parents would have insisted that everything possible be done to save their child. But Jim and I couldn't ask anything more from this battered child. He had endured more pain and procedures and side effects in his short time on earth than most people suffer in a lifetime. I couldn't ask him to endure any more pain or suffering. We gave him permission to choose what would next happen to his poor, devastated body. We allowed him the right to decide what he wanted for his life.

It would take me a long, long time to fully comprehend what just happened in that room. I heard the words. I felt the intense sorrow that permeated the room. My greatest fear was now going to happen. My baby was going to die. Now, nineteen years later, I still don't believe I ever truly understood the magnitude of what was coming. All I knew was that I had to do whatever I could to give John the best life possible, no matter how long that would be.

John, Age 5

John, Age 9

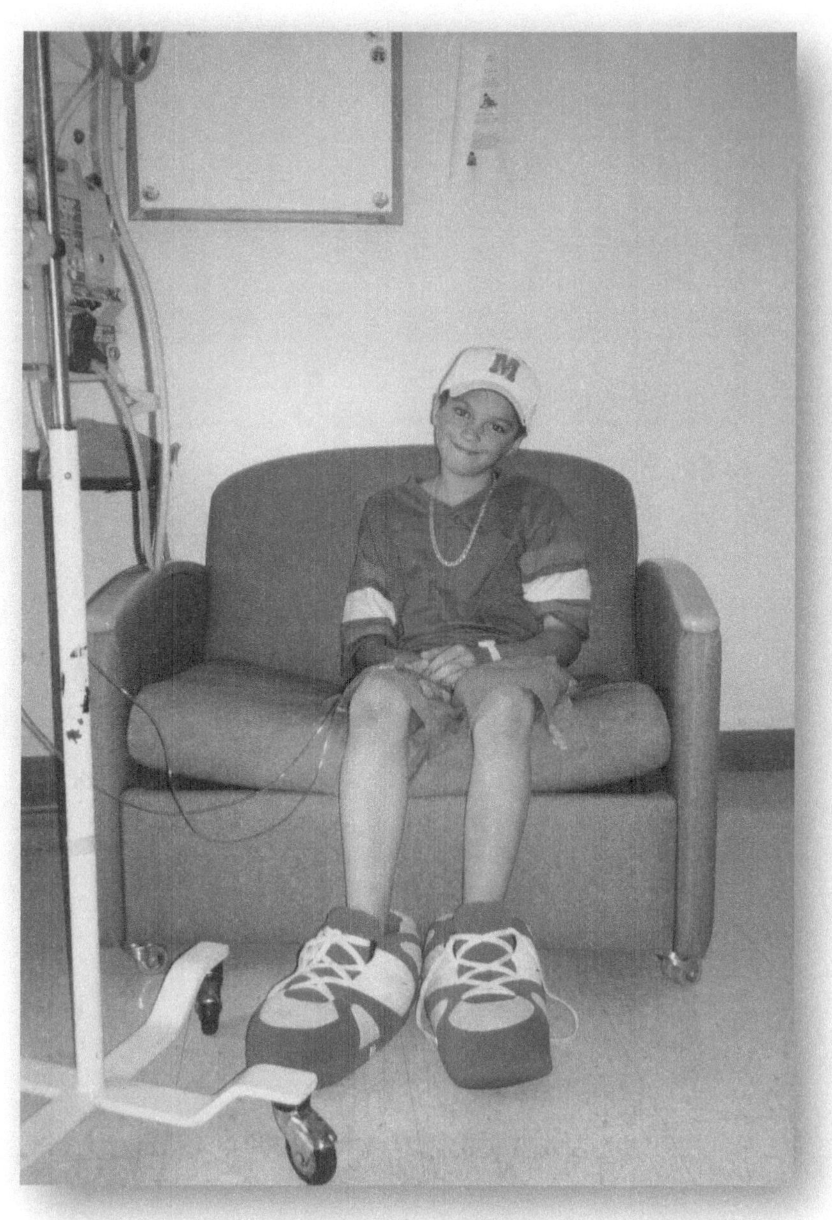

John's Favorite Slippers

John with His Cousins, Ben and Jack

John Enjoying the Playground Between Treatments

John and His Favorite Dog, Moo

John Enjoying Art & Crafts at Camp

John with His Friends, Brent and Keith, at an Orioles Game

John and His Siblings at Disney World on His Grant a Wish Trip

Wandishin Kids, 2001

John's Confirmation, 2003

John and His Date Chelsea Dressed Up for the Christmas Dance

John and Mom at Johns Hopkins Hospital

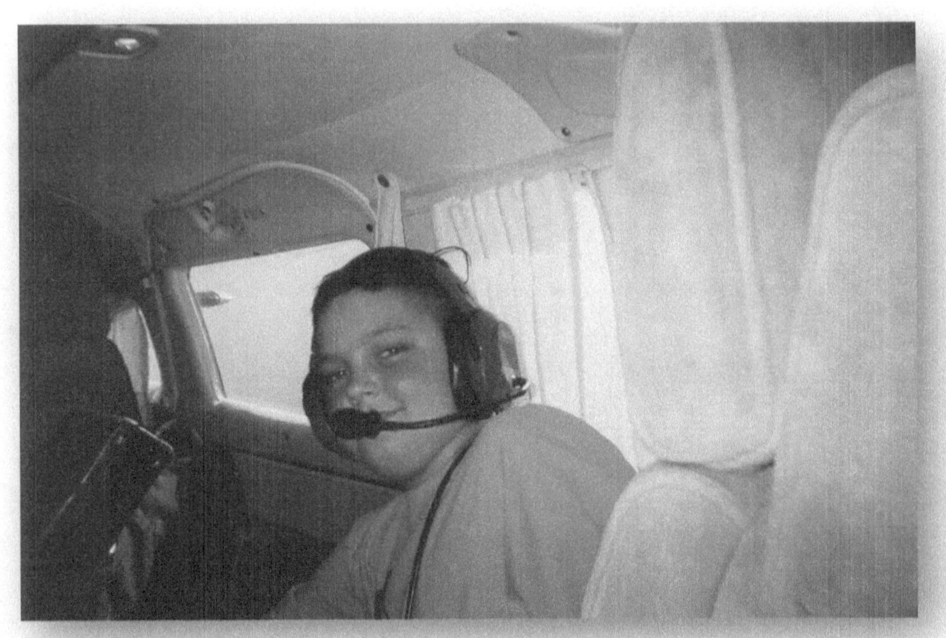

John on Angel Flight to Camp Sunshine in Casco, Maine

John at the Tennessee Titans Practice Facility

John Enjoying a Helicopter Ride

John at Camp Fantastic in Front Royal, Virginia, 2004

John and His Siblings on Family Trip to Disney World, 2005

Wandishin Family on Family Trip to Disney World, 2005

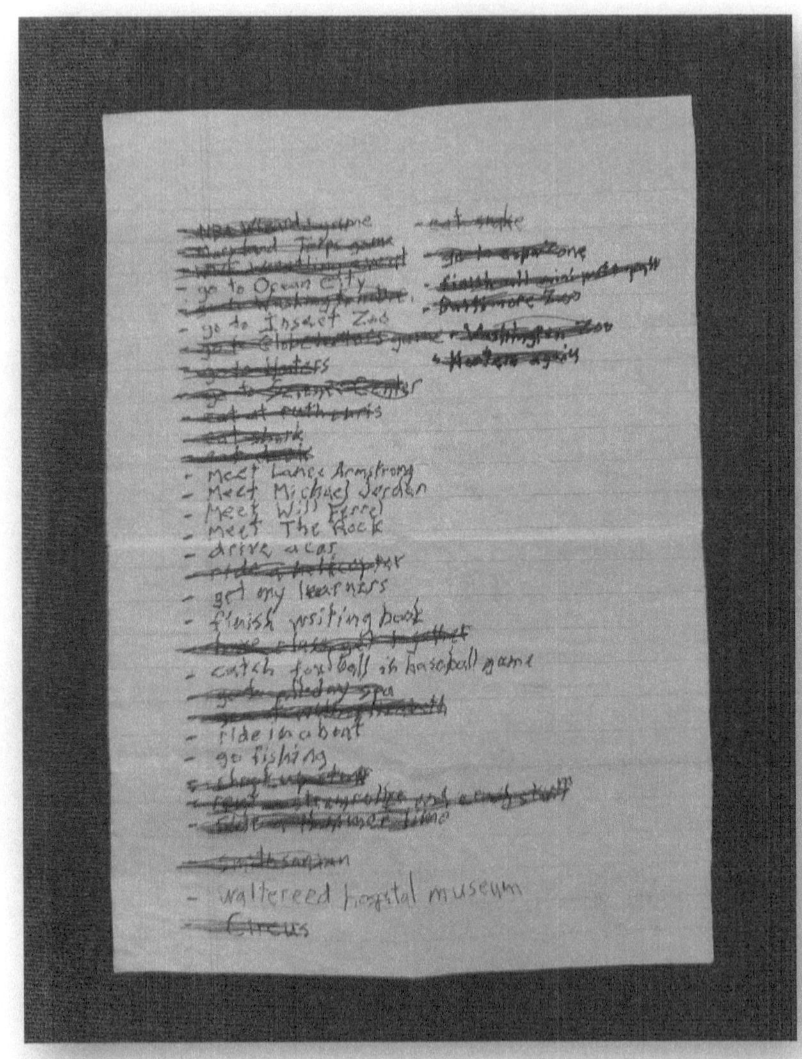

John's Bucket List

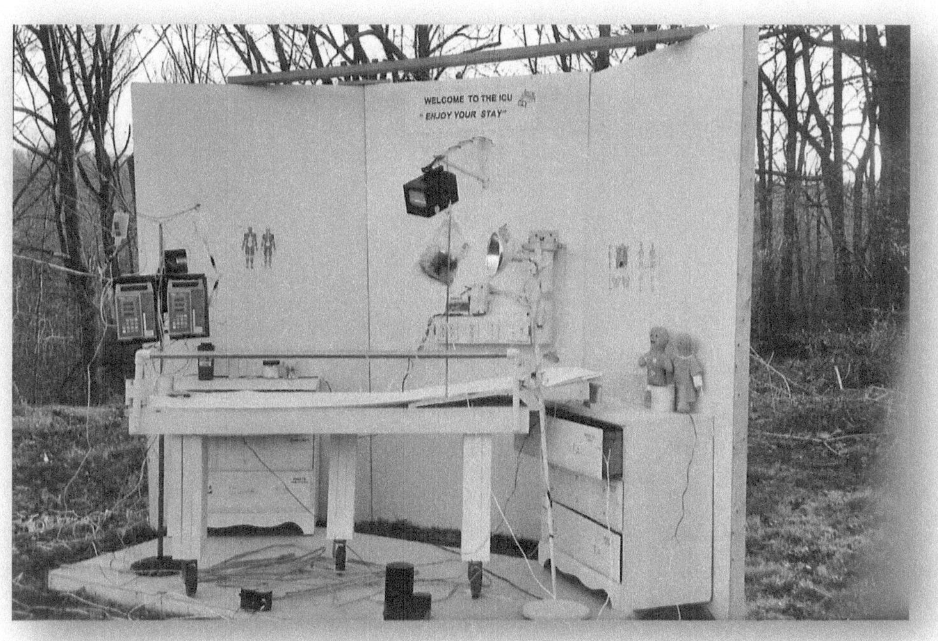

Hospital Set Created for Paint Ball War, Courtesy of His Uncles

The Wandishin Family, 2024

CHAPTER 16

Living Life to the Fullest

THANKSGIVING WAS JOHN'S favorite holiday. He just loved the traditional food of turkey and all the trimmings. He loved that the family gathered together to give thanks and share a meal. He loved the subdued nature of the holiday. It wasn't crazy and hectic like Christmas. It was calm and relaxing. It wasn't lost on any of us that this Thanksgiving would probably be his last. We relished every second of that day. I wished that every memory of that day would indelibly imprint its image on my mind. I didn't want to forget a thing.

In December John decided not to return to school. It was getting harder for him to muster the energy needed to get himself ready and then spend the day in classes. He didn't take this decision lightly. He loved school and embraced the normalcy of it. But he realized he was losing the battle for the stamina and strength to attend. I suppose he also came to terms that it really didn't matter so much anymore. He wouldn't live to graduate and go on to college. He wouldn't use his education to cultivate a career. He wanted to use the time left for things he really wanted to do. I went to see Father Michael, the president of Curley, and told him of John's decision and his prognosis. I asked him if John could receive his school ring now, since he wouldn't live to his junior year, when they were traditionally bestowed. I also asked him if he would deliver the homily at John's funeral mass. He graciously agreed to both. He and Mr. Barry, the principal of Curley, came to the house a few weeks later and gave John his school ring, which he wore proudly until his death.

Christmas approached, and we took part in all the usual traditions our family enjoyed. John wanted a laptop for Christmas. It was more than we could afford. A lovely anonymous benefactor from Hopkins got one for him, and Kim gave it to me secretly so John could open it Christmas morning. I treasured all these memories in my heart, as I knew Christmas would never be the same for our family.

In January our entire extended family—my four siblings and their families, my mom and my uncle, and our family—took a trip to Disney World. We stayed in two huge houses outside of the parks and visited a different attraction each day, including Universal Studios Park. The amazing thing about that trip is that all twenty-one of us did EVERY-THING together. Every meal, every attraction, every shopping trip was done together. No one broke off to do their own thing apart from the group. John had insisted on this. He wanted to experience everything with everyone! He didn't want to miss a thing and absolutely cherished each experience with his entire family. I don't remember who paid for this trip, but I know we didn't pay for anything, and I am grateful to my family for creating this unforgettable memory for us.

"Live Like You're Dying" is the title of a popular song by Tim McGraw that was out when John was dying. I cannot hear that song and not think of him. When John was out of options to treat his illness, he gallantly and peacefully accepted that he would live out the rest of his life, whatever time that was, as passionately, tenderly, and lovingly as he could. One of John's friends at Curley had an uncle, Rod, who worked with the Baltimore City Fire Department. He heard John's story and reached out to us and asked what he could do. We told him John just wanted to live every day and experience as much as he could. John had started a "bucket list" on a yellow ruled pad of paper, long before the *Bucket List* movie ever came out. Each day he would make a list of things he wanted to do, places he wanted to visit, movies he wanted to see, books he wanted to read, foods he wanted to taste, and people he wanted to say I love you to. Like a palate of splendid rich colors, each moment in his life held the promise of a smorgasbord of new adventures. As we accomplished one of his wishes, he would cross it off and add another. The yellow pad was never blank.

Rod from the fire department got busy and planned many outings for John. One was a trip to Red Brick Station, a local restaurant with a fire department theme. A brand-new fire engine that had not been put into service yet picked us up at the house and drove us to the restaurant, where we had lunch with the Baltimore City fire chief, Mr. Bill, and several other fire department station chiefs. They had a table full of gifts for John, including fire department-themed hats, patches, and shirts. Another outing was a trip to the ESPN Zone by limo for him and his friend Keith, and his cousins Ben and Jack. And yet another wish was achieved when we all went to Mo's restaurant so John could taste shark! We savored dinner at Ruth's Chris thanks to a kind and generous patient we met at John's photopheresis treatments. We went to the Orioles baseball games, Six Flags amusement park, and the zoo. John got to ride in a helicopter and went to a spa day, where he enjoyed a facial, manicure, and pedicure. We went to Hooters often—for the wings! John truly delighted in the attention he got from the Hooters girls! He was a teenager after all and thanks to his testosterone patch, his hormones were working just fine. John had thirty-seven items on the list. We were able to accomplish twenty-five of those wishes! John ran out of time to complete the rest. However, one of the things he really wanted to accomplish was write a book about his journey through cancer. I am beyond thrilled that finally this most important wish of his has come to fruition.

One of the most memorable experiences was meeting Chris Rock, the actor, and watching him direct one of his movies, *Head of State*. John and another young girl fighting cancer were invited to sit next to Chris in "director's chairs" and observe the movie action. Chris bantered with them, sometimes using very colorful language, and the kids were thrilled! We have an autographed eight-by-ten-inch picture of John and Chris of that day.

John maintained his wicked sense of humor and love of mischief all through this time. Kristin, one of his docs, was a Philadelphia Eagles fan. John loved the Ravens, but his favorite team was the Tennessee Titans. He wore Titan shirts and jerseys and even had Titan boxer shorts. Kim from child life even arranged for us to meet the Titans in Tennessee and we flew out one weekend, met the team, had lunch with some of them, watched their practice, and attended their game. One day we were out shopping, and John saw a pair of boxer shorts for the Philly Eagles. He asked me to buy them for him. I didn't really know why he wanted them, but I stayed quiet and purchased them. The next time we were getting ready to go to the clinic John was especially cheery. He had this funny smirk on his face, and I wondered what was up. When we got there, we waited for Kristin to come see him. When she arrived, she performed her regular exam and then asked John to pull his trousers down so she could check his GVHD rash. He pulled his pants almost all the way down, and lo and behold, he had on the Philly Eagles boxer shorts! Kristin laughed so hard and was genuinely touched that he surprised her with some swag from her beloved team.

Another time of almost unbelievable but clever mischief occurred on a trip to the beach. We had invited John's best friend Keith to join us at our friend's condo in Ocean City. Each day, John and Keith would go to the boardwalk by themselves. I allowed the young teens that freedom, even though I was secretly worried whether Keith could give John the care he needed. But off they went, John in his wheelchair and oxygen tanks and Keith confidently pushing him. I asked them each time they went out if they wanted any money and to my surprise, they always answered "No." I surmised that John probably had money he had saved, and Keith must have had money his parents gave him. Every time they came back, they brought with them stuff they had bought in the stores or prizes they had won at the arcade. I was amazed at their frugality in making their money last. It was only after John's funeral that I found out the real story. John often wore big, baggy pants. When they went out to the boardwalk, they had a ritual they performed before going to the arcade. Keith would park the wheelchair with John in it at a busy corner. John would sit on one of his legs, so it looked as if he was an amputee. They had constructed a sign that said, "Help the Handicapped" and gleefully accepted the donations of sympathetic resort guests. They had plenty of money to blow on that vacation, and John proved that he was resourceful and in charge of his life.

My three brothers own their own company called Image Engineering that designs and fabricates visual effects for the entertainment industry, such as lasers, lightning, flames, and special effects. My oldest brother John decided to create a very therapeutic activity for John. John was a new widower, having lost his wife, Marianne, to cancer the previous June. John, Joe, and Andy got to work and created a mockup of a hospital room. It sported a bed, fake IV pumps and saline bags, lights, monitors, a blood pressure cuff, and even dolls that the child life department would use to teach kids about their procedures. They made all this look surreally realistic, and it was contained in a three-sided walled enclosure like a movie set. They set it up on a hill on John's property. We were invited to come for a cook-out and then climbed up the hill for the show. Rita and Dave were also there; their daughter Katie had just died in March. John and Dave and Rita had become fast friends. I called them when Marianne was dying to see if they could stop by John's house and feed his cats. They lived right up the street. This one act of kindness led to a friendship that exists today.

As we took our seats, John brought out a couple of paint guns and gave one to John and one to Dave and Rita. He instructed them to point and shoot at whatever piece of the set they wanted. The paint balls started flying, splattering the mostly white set with red paint. Talk about a way to unleash pent-up frustrations! After the paint was exhausted, John was given an electronic controller. My brother pointed out a button and told John that he could literally blow up the scene with one push. John gleefully pushed the button and the scene exploded in flames and fireworks! It was glorious! As the flames died down and after enough damage had been done, they were extinguished. One last piece of business remained. Brother John drove his bobcat out and helped John into the cab. John was instructed how to operate it and he promptly bulldozed the charred remains of the hospital scene. What a cathartic, healing evening that was! I described that night to John's medical team the next time we were at the clinic, and they were all enthralled with the idea and wondered how they might (safely) implement something like that at camp.

As spring approached, I could see that John was gradually getting more tired and air hungry. We would gradually have to set the liters of oxygen up higher as his breathing became more labored. He got out of breath very easily and used his wheelchair whenever we went out. We continued to come to the clinic because I was frankly not ready to say goodbye to these people, this family that had seen us through the worst time in our lives. We were technically under the care of hospice now and there was really no need to go to the clinic. Hospice oversaw the dispensing of meds and ordering of palliative care options. However, eventually I decided with John in agreement that we would stop going to the clinic at Hopkins. I had finally realized that going to the clinic was about ongoing treatment. These families still had hope that their child could beat their cancer. It became difficult to hear how other patients were going on this therapy or that drug to battle their disease. We were no longer in the battle stage. We weren't fighting the war any longer. It was time to move on.

John was told that he could stop taking a lot of his medications if he wanted. It really didn't make a lot of sense to continue to bombard his body with all these meds. The complications we were trying to prevent didn't much matter any longer. We would treat minor infections with antibiotics, and it wasn't that important to support his heart or his kidneys or his cholesterol. After consulting with John, I signed a DNR (do not resuscitate) document on his behalf. No major support like a ventilator or hospital admission or CPR would be done in an emergency. John stayed on a few drugs, but mostly morphine. Morphine was the best pain drug that could also treat his air hunger.

John fully realized that the time he had with us was growing shorter, and he wanted the time to be peaceful and relaxed. He saw no value in wasting time on pointless arguments, squabbles, or grudges. So, he created a list of rules for our family and posted it on the refrigerator. Some of them were quite funny—like only using the upstairs bathroom when you had to go Number Two so the rest of the family wasn't subjected to any bad odors. Or that we all should have a picture of his favorite dog in our wallets. But most of the rules were gut-wrenchingly honest. Like, make sure the last thing you say to someone at the end of each day isn't anything you will regret later. Or no yelling at each other in the house. He wanted us to make time for one another and try to do something nice for each other every day. He wanted us to speak gently and kindly. He also fined us if we used profanity, and the money was put into an unused urinal to later go to charity. John reminded us of the basics of how to love one another. He demanded harmony among our family and our relationships and wanted us to experience the value of living in peace.

Our community of Essex, the Knights of Columbus, and our Church of St. Clare carried us through this most difficult time. There were several local newspaper articles that were written about John and several fund raisers were held to assist us with the medical bills. This village will never know the extent of our appreciation.

During the last two months of John's life, we did whatever he wanted. If he was up to it, we went on an outing or to the store to buy a movie or video game. If he wasn't, he slept a lot and ate whatever he wanted. Keith and Brent visited. John talked to me, but mostly Dot, about death. He went to youth ministry meetings with Dot when he could. He talked freely to the kids about his impending death, which wasn't accepted well from some of the parents of the kids. They thought it was too much for their kids to handle. But it was John's reality, and he had a right to share what was on his mind. Indeed, it was a hard, deep, intense topic for the kids to face but for John it was real. Evenings at our home during those months were fun. Family and friends would just drop by, and we would get take-out, especially John's favorite, steamed shrimp. We also had plenty of Mike's Hard Lemonade on hand. John had discovered the sweet alcoholic drink and delighted in imbibing. At one point someone asked if it was OK for John to drink alcohol since he was on so many meds. We just looked at them and smirked. Does it really matter now? So many things that were deemed so important before seemed pointless now. We were no longer trying to keep John alive. We accepted the fact that GVHD would have the last word, and waited for Sister Death to alleviate John's suffering and bring him finally to peace.

On the advice of Dot and Kim, the child life specialist at Hopkins who had had an enormous impact on his last years of life, John recorded a video for his family. He wrote his thoughts about each of us on that same yellow pad of paper. Chrissy recorded him reading each little speech, which described what we meant to him, how grateful he was for us, and what he hoped for us in the future. He was completely honest about his worries for each of us and how he hoped that we would not allow our grief to derail our lives. We watched it weeks after he left us. It was heartbreaking to hear how unsteady his voice was because he was struggling to breathe, and incredibly painful to hear him speak to us as if he was with us in the living room. At the time we owned five dogs. You can hear the cacophony of barking in the background of most of his video, and I know John must be smiling about that! We will forever treasure this everlasting gift he gave each of us!

Waiting for someone to die is a strange state of being. It's like I was in between time—time when my son was still with me, and I could love on him and the future time when he would be gone forever. It was knowing the train was speedily coming to run me over, but I didn't really know when that would be. I could hear the train horns and feel the earth vibrate with its rumbling, but I couldn't quite see it. My emotions were all over the place, converging all at once and confusing me. One moment I felt almost relieved that the time was coming that my beloved John would be finished with his suffering, and the next moment I was hit with an agonizing force of desolation, knowing he was leaving. I had never witnessed someone's death before. I was terrified of what it would look like and of the prospect of seeing my once vibrant little boy lay still and lifeless in death.

When the month of June dawned, I asked John what he wanted to do for his birthday. I told him we could have a big party, go somewhere special like an Orioles game or ESPN Zone, play video games, or anything he wanted. His answer surprised me. He said he didn't want to plan anything. Up to this point he had planned every day since we stopped treatment in November. He had written on his yellow pad all kinds of things he still wanted to do. I asked him again what he might want to honor his birthday. "All I want to do is sleep," he said. I presumed that he was just tired when I asked him, and I would ask the question again at another time. I didn't fully realize that he must have known when he was leaving us. That somehow, he knew deep within himself that he wouldn't be among us to have a birthday celebration. John was born on June 29. He died on June 28.

CHAPTER 17

One Day at a Time

THE TWO MOST IMPORTANT lessons I learned from this time in my life were: "Live each moment of every day as if it were your last"; and "One day at a time." One day at a time. ODAT. In the twelve-step community, this phrase is like a mantra. It is said at every twelve-step meeting and is used among the recovering almost as a greeting. Living in the moment one day at a time has proven to be one of the most valuable tools used to recover from addiction. The addict doesn't have to refrain from using for a week, a month, or years. They only have to navigate today without using their drug of choice. To the addict, and indeed to many of us facing difficult trials and burdens, looking ahead to the future is just too big, too much, too insurmountable. But to be able to do anything or refrain from doing something is much more manageable if we know we only have the next twenty-four hours in which we need to focus on it. When tomorrow comes, we can look at that day as only having to deal with whatever for twenty-four hours. And so it goes, one day at a time. We are only given one day at a time to live. In fact, we are given only one minute, or second, or nanosecond at a time. At any moment our lives can change in the most profound ways, and what we perhaps had planned for the future may never happen.

Lennon wrote in his song "Beautiful Boy" that life is what happens to you when you are busy making other plans. For the first year of John's illness, I maintained a philosophy that our family would just get through this and then we would live again. I planned our life and how we would enjoy it again only after John got well. Life for our family was on hold and would only resume once this nightmare was over. I was inherently a planner. I wanted to know what next week looked like or next month or next year. I wanted to achieve certain goals within a time limit I had set for myself and, if I didn't attain the goal within the time I had allotted to myself, I felt frustrated, inadequate, and insufficient. I looked ahead constantly to plan for events long before they were scheduled to happen. I wanted to know what was going to happen with John's treatment. I wanted to know if he was going to beat this cancer or die from it. But then, as that first year rolled into two and three, and beyond, I realized that life was happening right now, this moment, in the middle of treatments, drugs, and pain. John's illness wasn't an interruption of life; it *was* life. I needed to cherish each moment as it unfolded one day at a time and store those memories in my heart. If I always looked to tomorrow or beyond, I would miss today and I would have nothing in my repository of treasured memories to carry me through the difficult years ahead. As I would learn, those memories are sacred and life-giving and essential in bringing me comfort and hope as I begin another day without him.

John met each new day he was alive with enthusiasm and anticipation of what it might have in store for him. Even the most mundane of life's experiences held an excitement for him because he never knew when the time would come that he would not be able to experience it. Each moment of each day is a precious treasure. We have the choice to embrace it or ignore it. John taught me to not only embrace life but grab it with both hands with gusto and passion and shake every bit of enjoyment out of it. What would it be like if we all looked at the simple pleasures and blessings of each day as if it were the last day we would see them? I bet we would all enjoy more happiness, peace, and gratitude in our families and in ourselves. Don't wait until you are dying to notice and appreciate the everyday beauty of life! And don't wait to do those things you have always wanted to do. Don't wait to wear that special dress or try that restaurant. Don't put off going on that trip or taking that vacation or seeing that wonder of the world. You might wait too long and run out of time. I still marvel at John's attitude about life when he knew he was going to die. I was amazed that he fought with every bit of energy he had to enjoy his life, especially when it got hard to even get out of bed. What would you do if you knew your death was imminent? John, a mere teenager, taught all of us how it's done!

Chapter 18:

Rainbow Express Home

J OHN DIED EARLY ON A Tuesday morning just after midnight on June 28, the day before his sixteenth birthday. On the Friday before his death, we went to the Baltimore Science Center with Dot, Barb, Ben, and Jack. I bought him a large stuffed penguin he saw in the gift shop. He loved penguins! He had been collecting them for years. It was 24 inches tall, perfect for hugging. We then went to Hooters for lunch and to see "the girls!" When we arrived home John was very tired, and I could see he was struggling to catch his breath. He immediately went to bed to take a nap. That night, as I walked out of his room after tucking him in, he called after me. I sat on his bed and hugged him, and he said ever so softly, "I'm scared." I knew that he knew that his time was coming to an end. I told him it was OK to be scared. I shared that everything I knew from my faith in God told me that heaven was a wonderful place. He would meet his grandpa (my dad) whom he never knew since he died before John was born. He would be reunited with Kelly and Katie and all the kids he knew from the hospital who had died. He could play with his dogs that had previously gone to the Rainbow Bridge, and he would be well and happy. I added that once he got there, he would think why he (or anyone) was so hesitant to go.

I promised him that his dad and I would be OK after he had gone. I knew that children who are dying especially feared what would happen to their parents after they died. John was particularly concerned about what would happen to our marriage once he was gone. He had witnessed the breakup of a marriage of close friends who had lost a child.

On the New Year's Eve following his death, Jim and I were with Dot. After midnight, she handed me a gift that she said John had instructed her to purchase for me. Already in tears, I started to cry even more as she handed it to me. I imagined all the possibilities this gift could be, probably some sort of handmade gift of great sentiment and emotion. I slowly opened the package. I was speechless. It was a sexy nightie; one you might see in the Victoria Secrets catalogue! John saw great value, as only a teenage boy would, in ensuring that our love life was healthy and hearty, and therefore our marriage!

Saturday dawned and I could hear John's breathing was unusually loud and crackly. I called our hospice nurse, and she scheduled a visit later that day to take a look at him. John was very sleepy all day and did not want to eat anything, which was very unusual for him. He loved to eat! Jeannie, the nurse, came and listened to his breathing and took his vitals. She motioned for us to come into the kitchen out of earshot from John. She gently explained that she believed that John's time was very short now. The crackling we were hearing was what is usually called the "death rattle." She left, saying she would call later to check on him. I called Dot and my mom. They were both on trips. They both decided to come home immediately, for which I will always be grateful.

That night John began to vomit. He hadn't really eaten much during the day, but we were thankfully able to get his morphine in him. He was still taking it orally. I spent the night on the floor next to him and helped him each time he had to vomit. I didn't sleep. I listened to the rattle of his breathing and tried to quiet my mind as it swirled with the knowledge of what I knew was advancing quickly. I called Jeannie Sunday morning and told her that John needed a pump now, as he couldn't keep his meds down. Each hour that passed, John was experiencing more and more pain and air hunger. He was using his BiPAP machine with oxygen that forced air down into his lungs, but he really needed the morphine on board to alleviate some of the distress. We waited all day for that pump! We called our hospice service and the home care company we used every few hours for an update. I had heard that Hopkins was having trouble getting a doc to sign off on the pump. I was astounded at this incompetency. I can't understand to this day why there wasn't a standing order for a pump ready for the time when John would need it. They shouldn't have had to chase down a doc for the order. It should have already been done. The pump finally came late at night, around 9 p.m. John was miserable and restless. Jeannie came to access his port under the skin to hook him up, but she wasn't being very successful. I called Colleen, his nurse at Hopkins clinic, and that sweet woman drove forty-five minutes at 10 p.m. to access his port and hook him up. I just couldn't thank her enough. Finally, John would get his morphine and have his suffering relieved.

I kept my vigil on the floor next to John's bed during the night. Sleep evaded me again. I realized the next morning (Monday) that John's tubing had leaked on him all day. His bed was soaked and, more disturbingly, he obviously didn't get the meds he needed. Once again, we called Jeannie, and she came to fix the tubing. But unfortunately, John could never catch up on the therapeutic dose of morphine he needed to keep him comfortable.

People came to the house all weekend to say goodbye. Family members and friends kept vigil with us. Our dear friend Fr. Mike came and made us dinner on Sunday night. John's friends, especially Brent and Keith, came to say goodbye. It was so awkward for those poor kids. They had never seen one of their own friends die, or anyone for that matter. They just stood by his bed quietly. The girls cried and the boys remained stoic.

John suffered greatly those last two days. His body couldn't absorb the meds that were finally being delivered. He was in pain and breathless. He was literally suffocating to death without the benefit of drugs. At one point he asked me, "Why is this happening like this?" We had many discussions with his team at Hopkins, and they reassured us that John would fall into a coma and peacefully slip away. The drugs were designed to keep him comfortable and very much out of it as he made the transition. But it never happened like that. John asked at another time, "Why is it taking so long?" My heart shattered, and in utter desolation I replied, "I don't know." I was completely devastated. I could do nothing to help him. It was agony unlike anything I had ever experienced to watch him struggle and suffer so greatly.

Some of John's medical team, Meghan, Kim, and Nancy, came to say goodbye Monday evening. Dot, Barb, and Rita were already there, and my mom and sister Patty had come by earlier to say their goodbyes. The Hopkins medical team reported when they came into the house that an enormous rainbow arched across the sky, appearing to originate at the top of our roof. It was as if God sent it to light the way to heaven for our precious child. John was really struggling at that point. We could see that his feet and fingers were turning blue and were cold to the touch. He would thrash about, fighting for breath. Barb and Dot fiddled with the pump, trying to up his morphine, but by then it was too late. Our Hopkins friends stayed with us, as they could see just how much John was suffering. Sometime close to midnight someone suggested that I get into bed with John. As I lay there next to him, I could see that his eyes were fixed and staring. He seemed as though he had already passed. Suddenly his body started jerking and I became afraid and jumped out of bed and ran into Rita's arms. To this day I don't know why I did that. I felt so guilty that I left him! I struggled with this for a very long time and have just recently allowed myself to let it go. As I turned around, I saw him sit straight up and extend both of his arms out as if reaching for someone. I believe he took the hand of someone, maybe Kelly (Dot's daughter) or Katie (Rita's daughter), or my dad or an angel and went with them to paradise. He then turned limp, and someone eased his body back onto the bed. He was no longer in his body. He had climbed the rainbow to his home with God, the One who created him, the One to whom I had entrusted him and the One who loved John more than I could ever comprehend.

The initial emotion that washed over me was relief. Relief that my sweet, brave boy was no longer suffering. And not just the last several days of suffering, but the suffering that he endured the entire five and a half years he was sick. He lost so much and bore his losses with the strength and courage of a wise man. However, feeling relieved was short lived. Not long after he passed, the utter desolation that comes with the loss of a child came with the force of a hurricane and took my breath away. Never, ever had I felt such profound anguish and misery. I was inconsolable and my heart was crushed, knowing I would never again, this side of heaven, see John's cute face, hear his voice, smell his hair, or snuggle his body. I thought I could die from this kind of heartbreak.

We stayed with his body long into the night, until the funeral home came to pick him up. He looked so peaceful. The lines on his face reflecting the incredible amount of pain he had been in were gone. He seemed to have that funny little smirk on his face letting us all know that he was fine. We had made all the preparations for John's viewing and funeral in April. As excruciating as that was, I am glad we did. It made the next few days just a tad easier, knowing that most of those difficult decisions had been made.

The next few days are somewhat of a blur. The kids worked hard at putting photo boards together to display at the funeral home for the viewings. We met with the funeral home and made decisions about some smaller things, like prayer cards and the obituary. We went to the florist to pick out the flowers for John's casket. We had picked out a beautiful blue casket because blue was his favorite color. We chose his Curley jersey that the school had made for him with his last name on the back for him to wear. He had written a list of those things we wanted in the casket with him on the yellow pad. They included Rusty, his faithful stuffed raccoon he received the very first day at the University of Maryland. Later, I wished we hadn't left that stuffed animal in the casket—I wanted to hug it, hoping that it would somehow bring John close to me. We ordered Happy Birthday balloons to place next to his casket. The first day of viewing was indeed his earthly birthday. Jim and I each wrote a eulogy that we would deliver at his funeral.

The days of the viewing went by so fast. There were so many people. Jim and I never sat down as the line of mourners wishing to see us snaked out the door. I'm glad we had the customary guest book because otherwise I would never remember who was there. After the last night of viewing, only our immediate family remained with some of my dear friends. Dot and Melissa came into the room with a tray of tiny cups filled with Mike's Hard Lemonade! We toasted John, drained our cups, and placed a bottle of the drink he loved so much in the casket.

The day of his funeral was hot! The church was filled with hundreds of those who loved him and us. I could never doubt the love from our village! The young men at Curley who had carried John and his wheelchair up and down the stairs at school were his pall bearers, carrying my beloved son in his death. My brothers had put together a slide show of John's life to the song "Live Like You're Dying." Fr. Mike presided at the mass and Fr. Michael from Curley delivered the homily. Jim and I each lovingly gave our eulogies in memory of our amazing son. The music ministry, of which I was a member, beautifully sang the hymns we had chosen, and my friend Rhonda created lovely programs of the Order of Service. We buried John at Dulaney Valley Cemetery. We had already purchased two cemetery plots years ago for us. It was arranged that they would dig one of the graves double deep so John could rest there, and we would still have our spaces. The procession of cars to the cemetery was impressive. Rod had arranged a fire department vehicle to lead the way and we had a police escort. After the graveside service was complete, I could barely make it back to the limo. The lack of sleep and the horror of the last week had finally caught up with me. The church had planned a huge lunch for everyone when we came back from the cemetery. I stayed long enough to be social but couldn't wait to get out of there. I ate nothing. Finally, it was time to go home and as I entered my bedroom I collapsed on my ottoman and sobbed, "I want him back," I screamed, "I want him to come back." Dot and Diane lovingly helped me out of my church clothes and placed me gently in bed even though it was only about three in the afternoon. I knew I could sleep for days. It was finished. But, really, the real work of grief was about to begin.

John wrote this poem when he was only a kid in elementary school after his diagnosis, and this was printed on the programs for his funeral:

When I get up in the morning by John Wandishin
I want to be free,
Fly and be Soaring.
No I never want it to be boring.
I just push myself
To be better and strong

So I can have fun
And live my life long.
I always try to keep myself happy
Even if I write poems that are sappy.
I strive to be the best of my ability,
Even through the tough times
That my life gives me.
I think it's a problem
That no one can get rid of…
Help me Jesus,
I'm just a kid.

CHAPTER 19:

The Club No One Wants to Join

THERE ARE MANY BOOKS written about grief, and particularly the grief of losing a child. I have read many of these through the years and found them to be helpful in clarifying that I was not alone. So many of my thoughts and feelings were validated by reading the accounts of other bereaved parents' grief.

Grief over losing a child is not like any other grief. It is unique and its torment and misery cannot be compared to any other heartache. Our children are not supposed to die before us. That's just not what the normal order of things should be. In their innocence and pureness of heart, our children should not have to suffer such torture and pain. They should be free from such grown-up problems and be allowed to grow up strong and healthy so they can wage the battles they are sure to face as adults. They come from our own flesh. They are part of us, an extension of who we are. They are irreplaceable. You cannot just go out and have another child to replace the unique one you lost. They are that one-of-kind piece of your existence, sharing a blend of attributes of your body and mind. You see they have your nose or your eyes. They like things neat like you do or chill through irritations like their father does. No other relationship in the world is like the relationship you have with your child.

Another component of the death of a child is that their unrealized potential and unlived life experience dies with them. Your dreams for your child will never come to pass. John would never learn to drive as I white-knuckled the door handle of the passenger side seat. John would never date or fall in love. He would never wear a tuxedo or go to the prom. He would not graduate from high school, go to college, or get a job. He would never get married and buy a house or have my grand-child. The docs had told him that, because of all the chemo he had had, he would probably become sterile and never be capable of fathering a child. I wondered if this ever weighed heavy on his heart. I know he wanted to go to Hopkins University and become a doctor. I know he desperately wanted to have a girlfriend and feel the excitement and sweetness of that first kiss. And I know he wanted to live as long as he possibly could.

I stumbled through the first year without John in a fog. I cried every day. I avoided people for a while, except my close friends and family, because I knew I would cry when I saw them. There was no way I could explain my anguish to anyone. Only other parents who have suffered in the same way could possibly understand this misery. I talked often with Rita and Dot, who intimately shared this heartache themselves. Every holiday was torture; just getting through the day was my goal. It was impossible to share in the joy of Christmas without John open-ing his presents, or the comfort of Thanksgiving if John wasn't there to enjoy the feast. Jim and I left the house on the evening of that first Halloween. John so enjoyed getting dressed in costumes and decorat-ing the house for that spooky holiday. We couldn't bear to be in that gloomy house. I went back to my job at the church and buried myself in work. But it was so hard. There were so many memories of John at the church and parish school he'd attended. I began to plan my escape from there, and looked for a job elsewhere. My grief was just too fresh and raw, and the assault of memories was torture.

I began to dread the first anniversary of his birthday and date of death in June. I just knew it would be incredibly sad and I would relive those terrible days of one year ago. And it was just as miserable as I thought it would be. I cried all day for those two days and for days before. We had decided to plan a family outing to celebrate John's life, and went to Hooters for dinner one of those evenings. Friends and family members joined us, and we had a large table outside on the deck of Hooters and told stories about John. We kept this tradition up for many, many years. We attended Orioles games in John's memory or dined at Hooters.

I had to decline many invitations to cook-outs or parties with friends because I knew I would cry. My very closest friends were used to these outbursts of tears, but people outside of that circle would probably be uncomfortable. I didn't want to feel awkward, and I didn't want to be the cause of others feeling awkward. And usually once I started crying, I couldn't stop. Tears would form for hours or days from that initial deluge. I remember getting ready to attend a shower for one of Mary's daughters. I had a gift and was driving in the car on my way. For whatever reason I started crying in the car. Maybe a song came on the radio like "Live Like You're Dying" or I knew it was going to be the first time I would see some people I hadn't seen since the funeral. I don't remember what set me off, but the flood of tears washed down my face, and I called Mary and told her I couldn't come. I told her why and of course she understood.

I missed John so very much. We had become so close during the last years of his life. He was not only my son but my friend. We shared every day, every up and down, every exciting outing and every sleepy day at home. We talked about almost everything, except those topics a teen boy just can't discuss with his mom. He was the first person I saw every day and the last every night. His absence was enormous in my life. Everything reminded me of him. Dot had arranged for the hospital bed, oxygen concentrator, and bedside commode to be picked up the day after John died. John's room was drenched in his presence. His fish swam in their tank, his books were on the shelves and his horror figurines and baseball stuff, penguin friends and Hot Wheels, were displayed. His bureau and closet contained the clothes he loved, mostly sports motif outfits. The big stuffed penguin I bought him at the Science Center before he died lay in the corner. I picked him up and put him into my bed and I clung to him every night.

His computer sat on his desk with no one on the keyboard. There were no video game noises or constant hum of the oxygen concentrator. I couldn't hear his little high-pitched "hmmm" he used to express when he liked something. His fragrance was no longer in the room.

The sheets on his bed went with his body. You never think about those things. When a person dies, their body leaks fluid. And when they die at home, these fluids get on their sheets and the clothes they are wearing. John was only wearing a t-shirt and boxers when he died, and they went with him too. Mike's Hard Lemonade cooled in the fridge that he would never drink again. A DVD was in the player that he would never watch again. My arms ached to hold him and hug him and kiss his soft, thinning hair.

Not only did I miss my son, my friend, someone who was bigger than life; I also felt the absence of my role. I know I will always be his mom. But I was no longer his caretaker. I took care of that child 24/7 for all his fifteen years and 364 days of life. I bathed him, changed his diaper when he was a baby, fed him, clothed him, bought him toys and things that would entertain him. I took him to the doctors and dentist and barber. I helped him with homework and school projects, met with his teachers, and watched his soccer games. His care took a more intense and serious direction when he became sick. I learned to do all kinds of things a mom hopes she never has to do. I took care of his catheter, gave him injections, and administered so many drugs. I managed his oxygen, his infusion pumps, and lifted heavy tanks and wheelchairs into the car. I learned to navigate the confusing and completely frustrating jungle of medical insurance and hospital bills. I became competent in ordering medical equipment and supplies, and making sure we never ran out of anything. And, most heartbreaking of all, I struggled through the unimaginable job of helping a child cope with his impending death. I don't know how well I did that. I can't ask John if he felt prepared to die. I know I wasn't prepared. I knew it was coming and I thought it might not be as horrendous as I thought because I had had time to anticipate it and have the conversations I needed to have. But I'm here to tell you that you are NEVER ready to say goodbye to your child! As long as they are clinging to life in any way, shape, or form, they are still with you. You still get to take care of them and talk to them. But when they close their eyes forever, that's exactly what it means—FOREVER. I told myself that, since we had had eight months to prepare for his departure from us, the grief of his absence wouldn't be as bad; that we had been grieving a little during all those months before he died. That is just not true. We may have been grieving his expected departure from us, but as long as he was still with us, he was still with us! There is still hope, however shallow and false, that maybe he won't die. As long as he draws breath, he is alive and with me! But once death comes, that tiny sliver of hope dies too. The only thing missing from an anticipated death is perhaps the shock that accompanies a sudden death. But the grief of a death of a child is the same, whether it was sudden or anticipated. It is utter devastation.

After the first year had come to pass, I looked to the second year as being a little easier to bear. But honestly, it was worse. I cried even more and felt depressed and sad most of the time. Now I believe the reason for this is that we were told constantly that the first year would be the hardest, experiencing all the "firsts" without our child, first holidays, first family pictures, the first change of the seasons, and the beginning of each new month. The problem with this is that once we experienced and grieved through each "first," it somehow became a graduation of sorts. OK, we did it. We got through the first year. Now it will be better. But our child is still gone. Our child will still not be with us for those holidays and gatherings, the changing of winter into spring, wearing a Halloween costume, or opening a Christmas present. This absence in our lives is forever, not just for the first year after they die. I have heard from many bereaved parents that they, too, felt the second year was indeed worse than the first.

During the second year after John's passing, I was invited by several organizations to speak about my experience. I spoke at the Hopkins Annual Tribute Service for kids who have died under their care. I tailored my speech to the incredible wisdom our kids displayed and what they taught us during their illnesses and deaths. I spoke several times to medical students during their end-of-life seminar. John was honored at our local Relay for Life, and I gave the opening address. I wrote an article for CHIPPS (Children's Project on Palliative Care/Hospice Services) newsletter. I poured out my feelings and enumerated the life lessons John taught me. It was extremely healing for me to honor my son in these ways.

It was during the second year that Curley invited Jim and I to what would have been John's graduation ceremony from high school. Calling that moment bittersweet is a complete understatement. I was happy that Curley and his class would be honoring John. If there is one thing bereaved parents need more than anything, it's to know that their child is still remembered; that their name is spoken, and stories are told about their life. Parents never ever forget their child. They want to know that others never do either. We were seated in the front seat. John's portrait was prominently displayed on an easel in the Cathedral's sanctuary next to a huge lighted candle. His picture indeed was a focal point for everyone there.

As the graduates processed in during a rousing hymn played on the organ, a lump gathered in my throat the size of a softball. Tears formed and silently fell down my cheeks. He should have been here. He should be walking with his friends in their white dinner coats, solemnly marching toward their seats where, in a few minutes, they will receive the official document that proclaims that they successfully completed their studies and would now begin the next phase in their learning. He should be looking for me, and catching my eye, smiling in the charming, smirky way that only he could. Oh, the pain of his absence from the scene took my breath away. As we sat down and heard the graduation speeches, my mind had already created the image in my head of John among the graduates, halfway listening to the speakers and maybe fidgeting a little, waiting for the moment when he would receive his diploma. Maybe he was thinking about Senior Week at the beach and how much fun he would have and feeling the excitement of the prospect of truly being on his own. I was definitely NOT thinking about that! Perhaps his mind wandered to his plans for college and he felt a little nervous about the next phase of his life. I suppose I conjured up this scenario because the present reality was too painful.

As the names were called, I began to feel nervous. They told us when they called John's name, Jim and I should come up to the sanctuary to accept his diploma. I hoped I wouldn't trip or fall up the stairs and I could keep my hand from shaking too much. I hoped I wouldn't ugly-cry. The tears that had started at the beginning of the ceremony hadn't stopped and I knew it was a foregone conclusion that they wouldn't stop for that. We always had to wait a long time for our kids' names to be called if they were in alphabetical order since our last name began with W. Finally, the W's were being called and I held my breath. John Thomas Wandishin was spoken into the microphone. As Jim and I got up from our seats, the entire congregation rose to their feet. The cheers and applause were deafening and lasted long after we received his diploma and cautiously navigated down the stairs and back to our seat. By this time, I was crying so hard I couldn't see, and Jim grabbed me and helped me down the stairs. If it was even possible, my heart shattered again in a million pieces, and I wondered how I could continue to survive the loss of my boy. I recall leaving early before the final procession. I was ugly-crying by then and I didn't want to be a distraction to the hundreds of proud parents and their sons on this important day.

At this writing it's been almost nineteen years since my son left his earthly life and entered into eternal life with God. There are a few things I can say about this most awful loss and journey through my grief.

1. Grief is personal. Everyone grieves in their own unique way. There is no right or wrong way to grieve. For me, I found that allowing myself to feel deeply the sadness and giving into tears whenever possible was incredibly healing. I tried my best to limit my crying to when I was alone—in the car, in my bedroom, at John's graveside. It was just very awkward to cry in public. However, after the years rolled on and I became older and wiser, I really didn't care if my tears caused someone else's discomfort! That is one of the blessings of growing older. You can be yourself and not care what anyone thinks! I did break down and cry at my job or especially at church sometimes. I remember one Christmas I was at my desk and the Christmas Shoes song came on. You know the one—a boy's mom is dying, and he wants to buy her new shoes for when "she meets Jesus tonight." There was no controlling the tears that time and my co-workers either gave me a hug or kept a wide berth.

2. There is no timetable on grief. As outlined in many of the books I had read, grief is experienced in stages and a person grieving can

go in and out of the stages as many times as they need to heal. I personally don't believe that grief ever ends from the loss of a child. The dreams for your child continue every year he is gone. When John's friends each graduated from high school and college, it was a gut punch. When his friends started their careers, I wondered what John would have grown up to be. I was of course happy for them but how I wished John was among them! When his friends started to marry, I wondered what kind of girl John would have fallen in love with and married. When his friends started having kids, I longed to know what his children would have been like. Especially during my other children's weddings, John's absence was acutely felt by everyone. He should have been there, wearing his tuxedo and standing next to his brothers and sisters. Yes, I still grieve for him. I miss him most when the family gets together, and he is not among my other kids. My family of seven is now a family of six and I don't think I will ever get used to that. Our "us" is forever missing a member. But my grief has mellowed, and I have incorporated my grief deep into my body and soul. It is just as much a part of me as my arm or my love of dogs. I have learned to live with it like an amputee learns to live without a limb or a paraplegic learns to live without the use of his legs. I don't really remember a "me" when grief wasn't an integral part of who I am.

3. Do whatever you have to "fake it to make it." I changed my job after John had been gone for almost a year. It was time, as I had been there fourteen years. My kids no longer attended the church school and I had become bored with the work. Working there brought so many memories that were hard to manage, and everyone knew me. I realized that I needed to go somewhere no one really knew me. Where I could start with a fresh slate and decide for myself whom I wanted to share my story with and when. A new job would put me in a different light. I wouldn't be just the woman whose son died. My only identity would not be a bereaved parent. I would be just Kathy. I instinctively knew that for me to keep going and allow the healing to continue I needed to change my surroundings and

occupy myself with something new. Learning a new job would be exactly what I needed at the time.

4. Take extra care of yourself. Get enough rest. Eat regular meals. I didn't exactly eat healthfully and my weight gain after the first two years was proof of that. I ate what I wanted, usually comfort food, and I often ate with others, my family and friends. I stepped up my therapy by seeing my therapist more often and reading whatever I could find regarding grief, particularly from losing a child. If I didn't want to go somewhere, I gave myself permission to send my regrets. This time is ALL ABOUT YOU! Your body, mind, and spirit are going through tremendous stress. Going through extreme grief can cause all kinds of stress-related illnesses and compromise your immune system. People who are grieving are known to catch more colds and viruses. Get exercise. I started walking in the neighborhood even before John passed. It was not only healthy for my body but increased my endorphins to lift my mood. It also gave me lots of time to process my emotions. I found that playing some of the scenes over and over in my mind while I was alone helped in the healing.

5. Don't allow anyone else's opinions of how you are grieving affect you. It is none of their business. People who have no experience of something often have lots of opinions. Sometimes they say things that are insensitive and may hurt your feelings. Pay no attention to them and don't give their remarks any credence. This is your journey and only you know what is good for you. You will know if you are "stuck". If you believe that you should be past a certain phase of grief but don't know how to move on, seek out a close friend in whom you can confide. Get into therapy or join a support group of grieving parents. Talk to someone you trust, who you know has your best interests at heart. You can become "unstuck" and move through the next phase of grief, but sometimes you need a little help.

6. Do something concrete to honor your child. Maybe it's a donation in his or her name to the hospital or a society that supports children who have a specific illness, like the Leukemia Society or Diabetes Foundation. Establish a scholarship in your child's name to the school he or she attended. Become active in a group that supports

families who have lost children or families who are in the throes of their child's illness. For a while I helped Casey Cares in several capacities with their fundraising. One of the services Casey Cares is noted for is donating new pajamas to children in the hospital. You can honor your child with a simple donation of new PJs to this worthy cause. Or you can start your own foundation if you are business minded and come up with a new and unique way of assisting families during the worst time of their lives. My one big concrete thing to honor John is writing this book!

CHAPTER 20:

My Black Cloud

THE FALLOUT FROM JOHN'S long illness and death certainly took its toll on each member of my family. I wish I could say it was smooth sailing and everyone coped with their loss in healthy and meaningful ways. During the next twelve years, life was incredibly tough for all of us, each member of the family trying to find ways to navigate through the stormy waters of grief and sadness over their loss. There really is nothing in life that can prepare you for the assault of feelings that come with such a huge loss. We hopefully learn to control our feelings of anger, disappointment, and frustration as we grow into adulthood and find ways to channel these negative emotions into productive decisions or actions. We either learn this or we end up in jail! However, the topic of death and grief is still somewhat taboo in Western culture, and we are often confused and at a loss as to how to deal with our feelings of overwhelming sadness.

After John died and the swarm of family and friends all went back to their normal lives, I suffered incredible loneliness. The empty nest in our house came much too soon. All the other kids were already out of the house. Katie and Stephen were still in college, Joe lived with friends, and Chrissy lived with a boyfriend. Jim continued to work two jobs. He worked during the day at the US Postal Service as a letter carrier and did bookkeeping for our parish in the evenings, many times not coming home until 11 p.m. or midnight. I had gone back to my job at the church and came home to an empty house, and spent every evening alone. It was still summer, and daylight lasted outside until 9 p.m.

I often went to bed while it was still light out—I had nothing else to do, and sleeping gave me some relief from the crushing grief. I fell into the rut of going to work, coming home, eating something (mostly junk), and going to bed. The only people I talked to were folks at work and my dear friends who checked up on me. I didn't want to be a burden to any of my family or friends. They had their own lives and families to take care of. They had given me so much of their time and presence when John was sick. I just couldn't ask them for more time to help me deal with my grief.

After Stephen and Katie graduated from college a few years later, they each moved in with friends. I rarely saw any of my children except on holidays, and I didn't always see my daughters even on holidays because they were in and out of relationships with unhealthy people. My only companions were my five dogs—Winnie, Pumpkin, Moo, Binky, and Baby Dog. They followed me everywhere in my house and all of them slept on my bed. I was kept busy feeding, grooming, and walking them and it filled my need to be a "care giver," as I had loved that role raising my kids and even taking care of sick John. I honestly think I would have gone completely crazy without their devotion and constant presence.

I had accumulated five dogs really because of John. We had always had two dogs at any given time since Jim and I got married. I grew up with dogs and Jim knew that I would always have dogs—I would have written this in our wedding vows if I could. It was a non-negotiable rule of our union. The third dog came when our teenage kids went to Appalachia to rehab homes for the less fortunate and brought home a dog that would have otherwise perished at the hands of her owner. After John had been sick for a few years, he wanted a puppy of his own and so we adopted Binky. A year later, Dot wanted to adopt a puppy and John and I went with her to pick one out. Of course, John fell in love with another puppy and that one joined our pack. "John's dogs" were a soothing and healing source of comfort and joy for him during his last year of life.

My grief was all consuming and I felt utterly alone. I fell into depression and created for myself a victim's mentality. Up to this point in my life, before John ever got sick and died, I had suffered through the untimely death of my dad, who was fifty-seven years old (I was only twenty-nine years old when he died); three difficult pregnancies during which I was ordered bed rest in my seventh month and had to rely on family and friends to run my household and take care of my older children; a house fire that displaced our family for several months; and Jim's loss of his job of twenty years and subsequent unemployment. He was the breadwinner of our family, and his loss of income was devastating. I believed that a black cloud took up residence over my head and it would never leave. I perceived that every bad or difficult thing that happened to me was someone else's fault or God's punishment. Because I deemed myself a victim, I did not take responsibility to change my circumstances even if I had the power to do so. When I was unhappy in a job, I complained incessantly about it to everyone, forgetting that I did have a choice and could easily find another job. When I was unhappy in my marriage, I, of course, blamed Jim—it did not occur to me that maybe I was responsible for some of my discontent. When my kids were very young and sick a lot, I whined about that, never remembering that I had willingly and knowingly decided to raise five children and unfortunately being sick comes with the territory. I had come to expect that terrible things would continue to happen, and my dark cloud would never leave me. I could not catch a break. God must hate me!

Living with this pessimistic attitude drained my energy, leaving me excessively tired and disinterested in everything. I lived in fear, waiting for the next calamity to strike. Wading through the muck of my grief was bad enough, but to be constantly looking over my shoulder expecting another strike destroyed any sense of peace or well being that I tried to grasp. It took many years of therapy to examine my thought patterns and perspective to dispel the black cloud. I slowly stopped believing that God was punishing me or hated me. I read several books about the topic of bad things happening to good people and came to adopt the logic that God doesn't make terrible things happen to us. He is a God of love. He is our loving Father and would never wish calamity or tragedy upon us, just as we would never wish harm to our children. Bad stuff happens because we live in a fallen and imperfect world, and we are affected by the evil actions of others. God can choose to intervene if it follows His plan. Only He knows the big picture and what is good for us. He allows bad things to happen sometimes in order for us to grow and learn great truths. When my kids were all in elementary school, I would pack their lunches for each school day. Inevitably some child would forget their lunch and I would deliver it to them. Once in a while, the same child would continue to forget their lunch numerous times and it was getting more cumbersome for me to leave work and go home to retrieve it. I decided that the next time it happened, I would not deliver the lunch. Instead, that child would either have to beg the lunch lady for a sandwich and promise to pay her back the next day or ask a friend to share. I knew it would be painful and probably embarrassing for my child, but I hoped they would learn a lesson and remember their lunch in the future. The lady who worked at the children's lunch cafeteria was a friend of mine and I knew she wouldn't allow my kid to go hungry. The day came when my child forgot his lunch again and I told him I couldn't bring it to him. He had to ask my friend for a "loan" to get a sandwich. He never forgot his lunch again! I didn't enjoy knowing that my child had to suffer, but I knew the lesson learned would serve him well as he grew into adulthood, as there would be more important things than his lunch that he would need to remember.

The bottom line is that I don't know why I have had to suffer so many losses. I thought I had suffered my fair share of life's mishaps. Eventually I learned to trust God enough to let go of the fear and claim peace in the knowledge that He knew what I needed to learn and would keep me safe while I learned it. Of course, I had no clue what was ahead, and this trust I had cultivated and nourished to lean on God would become paramount in my survival.

CHAPTER 21

Choose Wisely Your Method of Coping

LEARNING TO COPE THROUGH difficult times is a lifelong lesson. There are many people who don't ever learn. I once heard the director of Catholic Charities in Baltimore say that one of the reasons why there are so many addicts and crime on the streets is that people do not know how to resolve problems. They turn to mind-altering substances to escape or pull out their guns to settle an argument. I suppose they think that avoiding their issues with drugs and alcohol or crime is the easy way out. The trouble is that when they come down off their high or run from the crime scene, their problems still exist and indeed grow bigger.

I get it. Sometimes it does seem more attractive to get drunk and numb out rather than to feel the sadness or worry or desolation of a loss in your life. But using destructive ways to cope will never work in the long run. If you don't walk through the pain and allow yourself to feel, you will never heal. Avoiding the cycle of grief prolongs the inevitable. It will keep coming back and biting you in the butt much later if you don't learn to address it when it happens. I have known some parents of whom it was said they were handling their loss quite remarkably. They were stoic and comforting everyone else at the funeral home. They hid their feelings of grief in front of everyone. They went about their lives, not skipping a beat. Later I heard that one or the other suffered a nervous breakdown.

When my dad died at the young age of fifty-seven, my mother was just fifty-two. She clearly remembers that on the night my dad passed away, a compassionate nurse told her that she needed to allow the tears to fall whenever they threatened. She should not try to be strong and hold them in. She should not over medicate to dull the pain, although anti-anxiety medication can be necessary in some instances and for some people. Shedding tears and allowing ourselves to feel the emotion is crucial in the healing process. Research has found that crying releases oxytocin and endorphins, which are the chemicals that make us feel good. They are also believed to release toxins and relieve stress. Strength is not about hiding our emotions—it is allowing ourselves to feel them and having the courage to share them with others.

Instead of making a potentially harmful choice to help you cope, try one of the following:

1. Talk to a trusted friend and share your feelings with them.
2. Do something that's good for you—have a spa day, go for a bike ride, or take a walk.
3. Do something you enjoy doing—cooking, reading, crafting, or shopping. (Just be careful with that last one—it is far too easy to spend beyond your means using "retail therapy." I know personally about this!)
4. Try a new hobby.
5. Keep going to church if that's your habit, or go back if you haven't been.
6. Pray—even if it's for a minute or two. Just touch base with God. Sometimes just saying, "Hi God, I'm here and I need you" is enough.

Denying that you are in pain, or choosing ways to avoid acknowledging it, is the biggest lie you can tell yourself! You are setting yourself up for a future of misery if you don't deal with your painful emotions. There are jails and mental institutions full of people who refused to acknowledge their grief and chose dangerous ways to numb the pain they felt.

CHAPTER 22

Down the Rabbit Hole

KATIE WAS MY WILD CHILD. She was the youngest when John began his long journey through cancer. She is probably more like me than any of my other children. Katie is high strung, easily excitable, and can fly off the handle at the slightest provocation. She is a perfectionist and prefers that everything be in order all the time. She was only in the eighth grade when John got sick, and probably needed her mom at that age more than any of the other kids. But I was often in the hospital with John during that time, and I know she was lost. Good friends took her out and bought her a dress for the eighth-grade formal, took her to her soccer games, and helped her with school projects. They tried to stand in my place as her mom, but it wasn't the same and I know that Katie not only felt abandoned, but guilty about feeling abandoned because she knew I was with John, who was seriously ill. She confessed to me many years later how she hated herself for her resentment that John got all my attention and time.

During those years I had hopes that Katie would not succumb to the reckless behaviors of her oldest siblings. For most of her teenage years I was unfortunately living at the hospital and Jim was working much of the time, and we weren't present at home for her. I later learned that Katie had started drinking at age fifteen and using pot soon after. I honestly didn't know. Neither her father nor I were home long enough to notice. After graduating from high school, Katie was accepted at Salisbury University on the Eastern Shore of Maryland. She lived there during the school year and got summer jobs in Ocean City, which was thirty minutes down the road. When she left for college, we had just buried John. To say that our minds and emotions were under the siege of profound grief is putting it mildly. Except for her grades, we had no idea how Katie really was doing in college or in her years in Ocean City. We saw her rarely and we had little energy to check up on our now youngest child. We rarely ever saw her, except for the few odd weekends she would come home to visit. Since she was doing exceptionally well in school and we didn't get phone calls from the police department, I assumed she was good.

Chrissy would visit her occasionally, and one day she came back and told us that Katie was drinking hard liquor as soon as she got up in the morning and would do so all day. Of course, I was worried and concerned and brought it up to her next time I saw her. And of course, she denied it even though I saw a lot of bottles of whiskey in her beach condo.

Katie graduated *summa cum laude* from Salisbury. She stayed at the beach for a few years to work. One day she called me and asked me to help her move back home. The next weekend I drove the van down and helped her move her stuff into it. I took her out to dinner, and she was in tears and looked terrible. She said she needed to get out of OC and get back on track. She wouldn't get into anything specific but said it was a rough atmosphere in which to live.

She wasn't home very long until she started staying nights away at her friends' homes. She got a job with Catholic Charities taking care of emotionally disturbed children. She loved it because she believed she was really helping those kids, but she wasn't making much money. She left that job to work for a musician; she specialized in advertising and booking gigs. She traveled with him, and I knew it wasn't a healthy environment for someone who abused alcohol.

She left that job and went back to work for Catholic Charities. She just couldn't get settled and appeared very restless and anxious all the time. She had a boyfriend whom I think I only met once or twice. Her taste in men was terrible! She picked the "bad boys," who were as wild as she was and made awful impressions on parents. This boyfriend lived locally, and she spent most of her days and nights with him. She was well into her twenties by then.

One night I came home from work and found her passed out in a chair. I looked in the kitchen and the box of wine I had bought only a few days ago was drained. I now had my evidence, and I knew she was in trouble. It wasn't until John's anniversary came up the following June that I knew the full extent of her trouble. Chrissy and I, Barb, Dot, Chrissy's girlfriend, and Katie met at the local Hooters to celebrate John's life. It was the night the derecho storm came through Maryland. I noticed that Katie was escaping to the bathroom often. She appeared very jumpy and nervous. The power went out due to the storm and we were left in semidarkness. It got stuffy and smoky in there and since the power never came back on, we left. Two days later Chrissy called to tell me that Katie had a drug problem in addition to her alcohol abuse. She was addicted to heroin. She had gone to Chrissy's apartment to try to withdraw and was horribly sick. Chrissy called a friend of hers who was in recovery and she suggested I take her to Hopkins Bayview Hospital for their withdrawal program.

I cried for two weeks after I found out Katie was on drugs. I felt like I had failed as a parent. I thought it must have been my fault, as I wasn't there for her early in her teen years. I later learned after much education that I was not the cause of Katie's addiction. She had to learn to take responsibility for that choice. I was terrified that I would lose her and would have to bury another child. I was so out of my element. I never in my wildest imagination thought I would have to deal with a child addicted to drugs. There were countless media spots and reading material out in the 1990s that targeted kids susceptible to using drugs. But these were kids from rough neighborhoods and broken homes. Surely our kids would never be tempted to do something so dangerous to their health. When I started attending parent group counseling sessions, I realized that drug addiction does not discriminate. Anyone can become an addict—those who have money and those who don't, those who have good families and those whose parents are absent, those who succeed in school and those who don't. And most of the parents I met at these meetings were just as shocked as I was that their kids were on drugs.

I drove Katie to Hopkins on Monday morning and registered her for their week-long withdrawal outpatient program. I dropped her off each morning and picked her up each afternoon. She was put on Sub-oxone, a drug that eased withdrawal from heroin symptoms; and Antabuse, which made the patient violently ill if they drank alcohol. At least while she was on this drug, I knew she wouldn't be drinking. I was able to get Katie into an eight-week-long recovery outpatient program at Sheppard Pratt Hospital. She spent every work day for eight weeks at this facility, where she had therapy, group counseling, and educational classes. Because she was in her middle twenties at the time, I was required to attend parent nights every Wednesday for group counseling and later attended an educational talk about addiction. I learned so much about this disease and what it does to the brain and why some folks become addicts and others do not. It terrified me to know that it was extremely difficult to kick an addiction once your body becomes physically dependent on alcohol or drugs. But it was invaluable information that has served me well through Katie's long recovery.

Katie completed her recovery program at Sheppard Pratt. It was August. I didn't really find out until November on Thanksgiving weekend that Katie was using heroin again. She had come home from her boyfriend's house and went to her old bedroom. I could see that she was struggling and as the hours went on, she developed chills, vomiting, fever, body aches and pains, diarrhea, and a host of other equally dreadful symptoms. Katie was withdrawing again. She asked me if we would help her get into an inpatient rehab center. I would have moved the earth for her if it made her well! She researched rehab centers and came up with a privately owned facility in Anne Arundel County. She called them and had an appointment for an intake interview in the morning. A bed was available on Monday morning! She announced her plans to my extended family at Thanksgiving dinner and we drove her to Serenity Acres Monday morning. It was no surprise that this facility didn't accept our insurance. It was privately owned and there wasn't as much money from the federal government as there is now. We ended up asking my oldest brother John and Jim's mom for a loan for the $60,000 needed for Katie to stay sixty days. Luckily, they never expected us to pay them back.

Katie settled into rehab life. She wasn't allowed to have her phone, so she couldn't contact her drug dealer or anyone with whom she used. I was so grateful for that policy. I knew for at least thirty days she would be free from alcohol and drugs and would be safe. Katie worked hard and spent much of the first thirty days dealing with withdrawal symptoms and cravings. She asked to stay another thirty days so she could continue the real work of changing her thought processes about herself, others, and God. Katie put 110% of herself into the intense work of recovery. She knew she didn't have another shot at this, and she wanted to accomplish everything she could to manage her addictions.

She journaled, read lots of books, got a sponsor, attended twelve-step meetings, participated in everything Serenity offered, and soon she was making plans to leave rehab. She decided not to go home but live in a sober living house, where other adult addicts live together to help each other be accountable. There are rules and curfews and mandatory meetings, but Katie knew that she needed this kind of support. After several months in the sober house, Katie moved in with two of her friends she had made in recovery. After several years, Katie and her sister Chrissy moved into an apartment together.

At the beginning of Katie's sobriety, I worried that she would relapse. I knew we could never afford for her to go back to rehab. We couldn't really afford it the first time and had to ask for help, and I could not go back to my family and ask again. I was most afraid that if she did relapse, she would die of an overdose. Most people who go back out to use again do die of an overdose. They think they can use the same dosage of drugs they had when they stopped. But their bodies have now lost the tolerance and if they use the same amount, they will overdose. I had to practice leaving this worry in God's hands, one day at a time.

Katie has been sober and clean for almost twelve years. She has channeled her exuberant and energetic personality into her recovery and strives for integrity and sincerity in all her relationships. Katie's vivacious and enthusiastic personality is one of her great strengths, and she is well liked and admired by all who know her. She has been a member of twelve-step programs since she left Serenity Acres and is passionate about helping others find new life after addiction. She has helped dozens of people find recovery and quite possibly saved their lives. She works for the Maryland State Health Department in the mental health/substance abuse field. She just married her best friend Drew, whom she met in rehab. Together they live a happy life in sobriety, honesty, love, and service to others.

CHAPTER 23

Addiction Is a Treatable Disease

NO ONE WAKES UP ONE morning and declares that they think they will become an addict. Addiction is a disease. People who are physically dependent on alcohol or drugs have different brain chemistry than people who are not. A switch in their brain is turned on when they take their first drink or drug, and they can't stop. My sons abused alcohol many, many times, but they ARE NOT addicts. My daughters also abused alcohol for years and they ARE addicts. I have learned that it is believed that the disease of addiction, especially to alcohol, is a genetic disease and is inherited. Jim and I both have had alcoholics in our family lineage.

This disease also changes how the addict thinks, and they withdraw into themselves, living only for the next drink or fix. They will lie, steal, and resort to behavior of which they would have never dreamed they were capable. The disease takes total control over their life, and they feel powerless over it. Most addicts suffer from self-loathing. They hate the person they have become, and they feel ashamed that they can't overcome their addiction. They have become a slave to their drug. And although they try time and time again to "kick the habit," they usually fail. It's not a failure of willpower. Their bodies have become physically dependent on having the drug in their system, and they get violently sick if they don't continue to feed their body the drug. They have a disease that needs to be treated, and the addicted person needs to get their thought patterns to a point where they acknowledge that they have this disease and need and want help. This usually occurs when the addict reaches "rock bottom," meaning that they finally realize that their life is in total shambles, and they don't want to live this way any longer.

People use alcohol and recreational drugs for many reasons. A teen will drink or smoke because of peer pressure. They want to appear "cool" to their friends and they don't want to be left out of the group because they are not using or drinking. Some folks use drugs and alcohol for a "good time." It's a social thing. Bars and restaurants with bars are plentiful and it is the top destination for adults to be entertained. But a lot of folks have found that alcohol and drugs dull the senses and initially make you feel euphoric or as though you haven't a care in the world, and they like that feeling, especially if they are emotionally hurting. Using alcohol gives you a break from the pain, a tiny little space of relief from the agony you may be suffering from the loss of a job, or financial stability, a home, or a loved one. The problem is that once you dry out and become sober again, the pain is still there. It hasn't disappeared. Your pain did not vanish, and you are not restored to feeling happy. You feel worse because alcohol is a depressant. And it all becomes a vicious circle of getting high and coming down until you realize you are drinking or drugging more and more to achieve a high because your body is developing tolerance. And if you realize you have no control over your cravings and your only constant thought is how to get the next fix, you are an addict.

I learned that addicts who go to treatment and espouse a twelve-step program and habitually attend meetings of other chemically dependent people and surround themselves with others who are serious about their recovery and want to live a joy-filled life free of addiction, usually stay clean and sober. As with any chronic disease, if the sufferer diligently follows the treatment plan, they can live a healthy life. But they can't do it alone and they can't do it without God. Yes, God. The twelve-step program is really all about God and how the addict learns to see themselves as loved by God. They learn that they are helpless and hopeless without God, and they come to trust in His power to direct their lives. When they truly realize that they are the beloved object of God's love, they learn to love themselves, and their desire to live a good life fuels their conviction to stay clean.

I now share the twelve steps with you. They are strikingly familiar if you are a Bible reader. Jesus talked a lot about the content of these steps and the need to have a relationship with Him. The twelve steps are all about our need for God to live a happy and joy-filled life.

1. We admitted we were powerless over alcohol (or insert any addiction or obstacle)—that our lives had become unmanageable.
2. Came to believe that a power greater than ourselves could restore us to sanity.
3. Made a decision to turn our will and our lives over to the care of God as we understood Him.
4. Made a searching and fearless moral inventory of ourselves.
5. Admitted to God, ourselves, and to another human being the exact nature of our wrongs.
6. Were entirely ready to have God remove all these defects of character (from step 4).
7. Humbly asked God to remove our shortcomings.
8. Made a list of all persons we had harmed and became willing to make amends to them all.
9. Made direct amends to such people wherever possible, except when to do so would injure them or others.
10. Continued to take personal inventory and when we were wrong, promptly admitted it.
11. Sought through prayer and meditation to improve our conscious contact with God, as we understood Him, praying only for knowledge of His will for us and the power to carry that out.
12. Having had a spiritual awakening as the result of these steps, we tried to carry this message to alcoholics, and to practice these principles in all our affairs.

If you or someone you know is suffering from the disease of addiction, please know it is possible to slay this dragon and live a life of joy and freedom. Reach out for help and give your life back to God.

CHAPTER 24

Lightening Can Strike Twice

WHEN CHRISSY FELL, it was a long, hard drop. In fact, she almost lost her life. It was Friday the thirteenth of January at 10 p.m. Jim had gone to bed, and I was watching TV in my La-Z-Boy chair. My phone rang and it was my son Stephen. He proceeded to tell me that Chrissy was found unresponsive, and she was being taken by ambulance to Hopkins Bayview ER. He said that he and Jennie were on their way to the hospital. They live in Mt. Airy, which is a good hour away from us. At first my mind couldn't process what he was saying. When I heard that they were driving down from Mount Airy at 10 p.m. on a Friday night, my mind finally registered that this must be serious. I still couldn't wrap my head around the fact that she was found unresponsive. What could that mean?

She was currently in a difficult, unbalanced relationship. She hadn't suffered physical abuse as far as I knew, but her partner was manipulative and needy. For most of her teen and young adult years, Chrissy was taken advantage of by this self-absorbed type of person. Before this person, Chrissy was in another relationship that was even more emotionally and mentally abusive. She just went from one narcissistic person to another. I haven't studied the psychology of abusive relationships, but I do know that poor and low self-esteem is a prominent piece of the puzzle. Chrissy didn't value herself very much. She was a beautiful girl. Her smile lit up the room. She was kind and compassionate as the day was long and always offered to help others in any way she could. She had incredible empathy for those who were suffering, and tried to "help" them. Unfortunately, many of these so-called "friends" took advantage of Chrissy's kind nature and Chrissy soon became the victim of their control. Chrissy was a people pleaser. She made the mistake many of us make by believing that if she did things that others wanted, they would like her. Her value was only worth how much she could make someone else happy.

We suspected that not only did she abuse alcohol frequently, but she was also addicted to drugs. Katie was sure that Chrissy had fallen into addiction to heroin. She could see the physical signs as well as the behaviors of someone on drugs, and of all people, she would know. We had a family intervention with Chrissy and her partner, but they vehemently denied it. They were high at the time of the intervention and still they swore they weren't using. There was not much we could do for her. She was an adult and free to make her own choices. I was sickened thinking that we were faced with this terrifying reality again!

On the drive to the hospital that night, I kept thinking and praying, "Dear God, I just can't go through this again. I don't have the strength." We didn't know if she was alive or dead. The hospital won't tell you those things. They just tell you to come to the hospital. It was inconceivable that we had yet another trial to survive, only I really thought I couldn't possibly live through this.

When we arrived at the ER, we couldn't see her right away. We were told the docs were still working on her. I hoped that meant she might still be alive. Finally, we were allowed in to see her. She was lying very still and sedated but alive. We were told that she had overdosed on heroin probably laced with fentanyl, based on the substance the paramedics found on her desk. It took them a while to rouse her with Narcan. She wasn't breathing when they found her and had no idea how long her brain had been without oxygen. They warned us that she might have suffered brain damage for the lack of oxygen, and only time would tell how much of her faculties she would retain.

I went straight to her bedside and sat in a chair by her head. I wouldn't allow anyone else to sit there, as if to guard and protect her from any more harm. I remember feeling oddly calm while I watched her breathe. I knew we were in for another nightmarish event in our lives, but I was resolved that we would do whatever we needed to get her back with us, in body and spirit. Her partner raced into the hospital room screaming, "It's not my fault. It's not my fault. I thought she had quit." We learned later that they both did lines that day. A surprising rage filled me. I have never felt so angry in all my life! I stood up and faced this person and told them to get out of the room. Chrissy didn't need all this hysterical screaming right now. And more than that, this person was not demonstrating concern for Chrissy; they were only worried about themselves.

After a couple of hours, Chrissy started to awaken. The doctor asked her what her name was, and if she knew where she was. She answered appropriately. However, when asked if she knew who I was, she failed to identify me. Stephen and Jennie stayed with us most of the night. Joe had come up as well to hang out with us. We couldn't get a hold of Katie until the wee hours of the next morning. She would know what to do. After all, we had all done this before.

When Chrissy was fully conscious, she instantly recognized all of us and I could see the shame and embarrassment all over her face. Her drug use was not a surprise to any of us, but her realizing that we "caught her in the act," so to speak, crushed her. She told us later that she also felt somewhat relieved. She wanted to stop; in fact, she had tried to stop many times, but the excruciating symptoms of withdrawal always won out and she called her dealer for another hit. Most of all, Chrissy was mortified that she had fallen into the same trap that her sister had and watched us go through the agony of her disease. And to be honest, we all were quite astonished that Chrissy had gone down that road.

She was the oldest and wore well the mantle of responsibility and leadership that comes with it. Several years before John fell ill, we had a house fire. On a cold, rainy day in February, I collected the four kids when they were dismissed after school, and we drove to the Doctor Pet Store to purchase a white mouse. It was Science Fair time and Chrissy's project involved our hamster and a white mouse. She had built a wooden maze, and the experiment was to see who was smart enough to get through the maze first—the hamster or the mouse. After we bought the mouse, I drove home and dropped the four kids off. I had to pick up John, who was two at the time. Chrissy was almost twelve and she had demonstrated that she could watch over her siblings for short times. I drove to the house of my friend Sharon, who was taking care of John when I went to work. I took my time and sat and talked to her a while, then collected John and started home. At the top of Myrth Avenue, the cross-street to Mace Avenue, I had to stop to allow several fire engines to make the left turn. I watched them then turn right onto my street. I had the thought most people must have if they see a fire engine drive onto their street: "I hope it's not my house!" I followed the engines up my street, and in utter shock and horror found that they had stopped directly in front of my house! I noticed that there were at least three engines on my street near my house, and the fire fighters were walking in and out of my house. I screeched to a stop with John still in his car seat and ran from the van screaming, "My kids! My kids!" My neighbor Susan ran from her house shouting: "They are OK! They are with me!" I ran immediately to her and embraced each of my kids. I noticed as well that my two dogs were also safe in her house. I called Jim at work to tell him that the house was on fire. At first, he didn't believe me. I had to stress the fact that it wasn't just a little fire and he had to come home.

After the fire was out, the firefighters came to get me and took me into the house to show me the damage. The kitchen was a total loss. Everything had either burned or melted. There were big holes in several walls, as the fire fighters had to make sure the fire wasn't still smoldering in the walls. The rest of the house was black with soot—every wall, piece of furniture, and knick-knack was covered in a black film of ash. Every article of clothing, bed linen, towel, and soft good smelled like smoke. Every step I made, the carpet sloshed under my feet, soaked with water. In my shock, I thought we could still live there and just not use the kitchen! I quickly realized we could not live in our house in its condition. We were told to gather some clothing for each person and whatever we might need and find somewhere to stay for the night. Jim and I stayed with Barb; Chrissy and Joe stayed with Susan; and Katie and John and the dogs went to stay with my mom.

The next day we came back to the house and waited for the insurance company representative to come by and assess the damage. I remember sitting on my front steps and crying, still trying to process what had happened and wondering what we needed to do next. I was incredibly thankful to God that my kids and animals weren't hurt, and felt so guilty that I had left them alone for just that little while.

We learned from the kids how the fire started. The children were all upstairs reading books and trying to sell some of them to each other. They were all quite resourceful! Katie had gone into the kitchen to get a snack before she went upstairs. There was a tray of snacks on the counter I had just bought at Sam's Club. She needed to climb onto the counter to get the snack she wanted in the cabinet. The tray was in her way, so she pushed it away onto the stove top. After she got what she wanted, she went upstairs to be with her siblings. The stove top had its knobs and controls on the same horizontal plane as the burners. The tray was pushed hard enough that it knocked up against the knobs and turned the burners on. The fire quickly started and burned the tray. The flames got to the smoke detector right outside of the kitchen and it went off. The kids heard it upstairs and Joe was voted to go down to investigate. He saw the kitchen in flames and noticed that the white mouse we had just bought was on the kitchen table. Stupidly he ran into the room and grabbed the mouse in its little box. He ran upstairs to alert his siblings that the house was on fire. Chrissy immediately went into action and told everyone that they had to get out. Katie was protesting because she didn't have shoes on. She was only five. Chrissy told her she would be fine and hustled all the kids out the door. They went next door to Susan's, but she wasn't home either. Her two kids were home and they were the same ages as mine. They attempted to dial 911 from there. Maybe they dialed incorrectly, or it sounded like a prank, but the operator gave them a hard time and hung up on them. They tried again and finally the operator believed them and sent the fire department. This must have taken some time because the fire was raging by the time the fire department arrived to put it out.

We stayed at my mom's for a few days and then Jim's parents offered their house to us. They were away on a trip and said we could live there, even after they returned, as long as we needed. It took four months to repair our home and we were finally able to move back in.

Chrissy was awarded a hero medal from the Girl Scouts. She acted responsibly and did everything she had been taught to do to get her siblings to safety. We were so proud of her!

Meanwhile, at the hospital, her "friend" had returned to Chrissy's hospital room and was going to stay the night. Jim and I, being assured that Chrissy was OK—she seemed completely herself and was entirely mentally appropriate—left the hospital at about 4 a.m. and began planning what we would do when Chrissy was discharged later that day.

With Katie by our side, we came up with a plan. We drove Chrissy home to our house. We had told her previously that she would not be returning to her apartment. Katie was already waiting for us when we arrived home. With Chrissy sitting next to her, Katie called and told the "friend" that they were not welcome in our house at this time. This was about our family now. The boys, Joe and Stephen, came over and once again, we gathered to show our support for one of our hurting family members. We told her that we would do everything in our power to help her get well but she had to do the hard work that comes with recovery. Joe, in his very direct way, told Chrissy that she needed to begin her recovery now, and that meant giving up any relationship she had that was contributing to her addiction. With Katie next to her, Chrissy called her "friend" and broke off their relationship. Katie was able to find Chrissy a bed at Tranquility Woods, another rehab center in Anne Arundel County, very similar to Serenity, where Katie had gone. And of course, they didn't accept Chrissy's insurance and we had to beg and borrow from our family. My brothers graciously lent us the $30,000 so that Chrissy could stay thirty days. And, again, they refused repayment, calling it a gift. I don't know where we would have been without the support of our family!

We weathered the weekend, never leaving Chrissy alone, and cared for her while she began withdrawal. Her amazing lifelong friends from the time she was in elementary and high school all came to visit her— Stan, Christa, Sharon, Maria, Erin, and Heather. I called them the "OG." How grateful I was for them! They didn't judge her or chastise her behavior. They just loved her.

Jim and I, Barb, and Sharon delivered Chrissy to Tranquility on Monday morning. She had nothing of her own with her. We wouldn't let her go back to her apartment, so she had no clothes, toiletries, or shoes. I lent some of my clothes and shoes to Chrissy and after we dropped her off at Tranquility, we went to the closest Target to buy her some clothes and items she needed for the next thirty days.

Throughout all of this, I was amazed at how calm I felt. I absolutely felt the presence of God through me, assuring me that it would all be OK. He gave me the strength and courage to walk another extremely rocky road, and each step I took I felt His love. Everything had fallen into place—we were successful at keeping Chrissy away from her "friend" until she was safely inside rehab. We had taken away her phone so she couldn't contact any of the people with whom she had used. The treatment center would have done it anyway. Chrissy fell into the routine of rehab life, finished withdrawal, and began the work of exploring herself and her God into recovery. She finally allowed herself to explore the burden she had been carrying for thirteen years—she blamed herself for John's death. Even though the doctors and our family continually told her that John's death was not her fault and that she, in fact, granted him more time with us by donating her marrow, Chrissy didn't believe it. She had told herself the lie that her marrow wasn't good enough and that was why John died. With the help of a wonderful therapist, Chrissy was able to work through the lie she told herself for so long and slowly begin to believe the truth.

Chrissy was ready to continue her recovery outside the rehab center, and went to live in a recovery home with other women who were in different stages of their sobriety. Chrissy could have come home with us, but believed, as her sister did, that she needed this experience to assist her in holding herself accountable and to later appreciating living a sober life.

Chrissy's story is truly a tale of resurrection from death. Modern medicine brought her back to physical life after her overdose, but she also gained new life spiritually and mentally as she climbed out of the dark depths of addiction where she had lost herself to embrace a new life of purpose, clarity, and authenticity. She met Mike in a twelve-step program and married him in a beautiful, joyful ceremony. At the age of forty-three she recently gave birth to a gorgeous baby girl named Anna Kathleen. She works as a speech therapist, and I have the great honor of taking care of little Anna while she works. Chrissy is my oldest child, the one who fulfilled my lifelong dream of becoming a mom. She is one of the sweetest, kindest, and most loving people I have ever known. While she holds true to her own convictions, she is also very open-minded and welcoming to those who may not share her beliefs. I feel incredibly honored and privileged to be not only her mom, but her friend. Chrissy continues working on her twelve steps and tells her story to others in the hopes that they, too, will seek recovery.

Chapter 25

God Never Said We Have to Like Everyone

GOD COMMANDED THAT we love everyone. And by love, I believe He meant that we should never harm anyone or wish them any harm—that we should wish for them good things, maybe even pray for them to receive blessings. Praying for someone who has hurt you is extremely hard. However, I have personally known this to be the best way to dispel your anger against them. Carrying around a lot of anger for someone is exhausting and blocks us from seeing so much good in our lives.

We must love all people. But God never said we had to like them, or especially have a relationship with them. There are some people to whom we may be attracted whom we should never have in our lives. Both my daughters and I have been in relationships that were toxic to us. Because we all suffered from poor or low self-esteem, we became attracted to a certain type of person who was good looking and charming and gave us lots of attention. These people showered us with compliments and gifts and took us on trips and vacations we otherwise could not have afforded. They also shared a sad or tragic story about their past or alluded to a mysterious disease from which they were suffering to gain our sympathy and appeal to our kind nature. If we felt sorry for them, we would do all we could to help them. Maybe we could "fix" them with our love. Before we knew it, we had fallen hard for these people. All we wanted was to feel valuable and special to someone. We just wanted to be loved.

I will tell you that when you are deeply entrenched in a relationship, when you are most vulnerable and when you are in terrible emotional pain, you cannot see that it is wrong for you. You believe that this person loves you and is giving you exactly what you need. Your friends and your family might tell you constantly that this person is taking advantage of or trying to control you, but you believe that they don't see what you see. You reason that if they knew this person the way you did, they would not tell you such things. You are blind to the truth.

Once we were in an established relationship with these people, they stealthily began to control and manipulate us. We heard them say to us often, "You would do this if you loved me"; "If you don't do this, I will find someone who will"; "I am the only one who can give you what you need"; and "You will never find anyone else who loves you like I do." They got angry if we went out with someone else, even if it was just a friend or family member. They would tell false stories about people we knew or loved, hoping that we would choose not to hang out with them any longer. If we got the courage to tell them that maybe they had an emotional problem and needed help, they would turn it around and say anything to make us believe that, instead, we had the problem. And if we told them we wanted out of the relationship, they became hysterical and threatened to harm themselves or commit suicide.

For my daughters, these relationships had a lot to do with their decision to use heroin. For me, I was in profound grief, feeling terribly lonely and wanting attention.

Thankfully, we all managed to extract ourselves from these people. One of us had to change our phone number and another had to threaten to get a restraining order against them. It was so hard to leave. We did love them, or thought we did. We had tried to leave several times before, only to return to prevent them from killing themselves, or so we thought. These people are all quite alive today! The one thing that we all had was the undying support of those who really loved us. They carried each of us until we could finally stand on our own.

I hear from my kids' friends that this type of abusive relationship happens way too many times, mostly to women. So many women tend to value themselves very little and believe that they will only be completed by the love of someone else.

We all want to be loved in a special way by someone. However, we don't need it to be whole. We are enough! We are enough just the way we are. We do not need to change or bend or transform for anyone. It should be our own choice to change. If we make a change, it is to better ourselves for ourselves and our God—not for anyone else. I do believe we grow when we change, but the growth is for ourselves and to be the person God created us to be. It should never be done to please someone else or try to make them love us.

The only person who can truly fix another person is God. We cannot heal whatever is emotionally broken in someone. Only God heals. If we use this as an excuse to be with a toxic person, we are kidding ourselves. It might sound like an altruistic reason to be with someone, but it is foolish to believe that we can do for them what no one else ever has been able to accomplish. We make ourselves out to be God and this excuse becomes our rationale to continue the relationship.

Look for the red flags! During my experience, I often imagined a red flag waving behind my head, not quite all the way visible. I knew that something was not right, but I was involved too deeply to take it seriously. The verses in the Bible that describe real love are in Corinthians 13:4–8, the one read at many weddings. "Love is patient, love is kind. It does not envy, it does not boast, it is not proud. It does not dishonor others, it is not self-seeking, it is not easily angered, it keeps no record of wrongs. Love does not delight in evil but rejoices with the truth. It always protects, always trusts, always hopes, always perseveres. Love never fails." If your significant other is treating you differently than the love that is spelled out in this verse, they do not love you. Move on.

CHAPTER 26:

Send in the Clowns

JOE IS OUR FAMILY comic. His sense of humor is epic. When he is around, you can be sure you will laugh. Joe obviously did his fair share of drinking as a teen and young adult. I found his stash of liquor one day when I was cleaning his room. He kept it in the middle of his pile of stuffed monkeys. When I asked him about it, he gave the popular excuse, "Oh, it's not mine. I'm just holding it for someone."

One time he was past curfew, and I heard his friend pull up to the house in the wee hours of the morning. I met Joe at the door, completely wasted, his vomit all over his shirt and talking nonsense. He was leaving the next day to attend a youth work camp sponsored by the Church. They were going to build improvements or repair houses for the poor folks who lived in Appalachia. He hadn't packed anything, and we were leaving before dawn in a few hours. I just let him go to bed and told him to set his alarm so that he had some time to pack. He paid dearly for his copious imbibing that night. He didn't pack any socks or contact solution and he only brought the underwear he was wearing. He lay in the back of the van moaning in the throes of his hangover. It was a four-hour drive to the workcamp with several stops. He was miserable, and a life lesson was learned.

When I told Joe that I was writing this book and that I really didn't have any terrible stories to tell about him, he quickly said, "You just don't know of my stories!"

Joe has been married to the love of his life, our wonderful daughter-in-law Katie. They have two children, Violet and Charlie. Joe is a mortgage lender and works extremely hard to provide for his family. He is a great dad, coaching Violet's soccer, basketball, and lacrosse teams, and active in her school activities. Charlie is only four months old at this writing, and Joe is already dreaming of watching him play in a variety of sports and share in his father's love of the Baltimore baseball and football teams, the Orioles and Ravens. Joe is amazingly creative, and he infuses his sense of humor into the media he has produced to sell his product. Joe is steadfast in his faith in God and rock solid in his moral compass. He is well admired and respected among his co-workers and friends, and his integrity and honesty are second to none. I worked a few months for his mortgage company and when I came in for the interview, I was greeted with, "We are so happy to meet the person who created this amazing human being!"

CHAPTER 27:

Laughter Is the Best Medicine

FINDING HUMOR IN THE worst situation a parent can experience is very difficult, if not impossible. There is nothing funny about watching your child suffer from a life-threatening disease. However, I am constantly astounded by the resilience and hopeful spirit sick children and their parents possess. I remember commenting to one of John's doctors that I was surprised at the amount of laughter I heard on the oncology floor. Instead of despair and sorrow, I found humor and hope among these families. Here they were enduring the most nightmarish months and years of any parent's life, and they laughed and joked and encouraged each other with optimism and hope. Rita and Dave's daughter Katie used to spend time making up David Letterman's Top 10 list—You know you've been in the hospital too long if…. Hospital Bingo was held every Wednesday in the Children's Center. Emesis basins were used to hold the kids' markers and the cards were a grid of hospital items. Emesis basins were used for a lot of other things as well, besides holding puke.

There is a charitable foundation called Songs of Love that creates songs for sick children. The child gets to pick the genre and fill out a questionnaire of the name of their friends, what pets they may have, their hobbies and favorite things, and Songs of Love creates a personalized song about them. John loved rap music and filled out his form. A few weeks later we received his CD of his very own song. It was brilliant, perfectly capturing John and all he loved. The night before the funeral,

Jim, the kids, and I were sitting in the kitchen, thoroughly exhausted from two full days of John's viewing. Suddenly, I heard John's song on our CD player and John and Stephen came processing into the kitchen swinging an extension cord with a stuffed animal on the end. They were spoofing an acolyte at a traditional Catholic mass swinging the incense on a chain in procession. They were not trying to be sacrilegious, but the idea of playing John's rap song in church was quite funny.

There were many tributes written by those who knew John at the time of his death. Most of the remarks were comments about John's sense of humor during the time he was battling his disease. His teachers, doctors, nurses, the parents of his friends, and his buddies commented on his exceptional ability to make jokes and sarcastic remarks amid his suffering. They mentioned that his smirky smile and hearty laugh was an inspiration to them, teaching them to not take themselves and life too seriously. John showed by his example how to lighten up even the darkest of places and maintain a positive and cheerful outlook during life's saddest and gloomiest experiences.

Poking fun at ourselves or a situation will lighten any circumstance. Laughing increases our endorphins and releases stress. I could have never imagined living through the last twenty-five years without humor and silliness. I would have already died from depression if my funny family hadn't lightened the mood once in a while with fun and laughter.

CHAPTER 28

For Better, For Worse Is Not a Suggestion

THE TRAGEDY OF JOHN'S illness and death, and the illnesses of both our daughters, took a huge toll on our marriage. For a decade or more, Jim and I were truly the proverbial ships passing in the night. We barely saw one another. When John was battling his disease, I spent every hospital admission with John, which could be from a few days to a few months. Jim was working two jobs Monday through Saturday. When John was home, I literally said hello to Jim when he came home from the post office job and goodbye when he left for the church job an hour later. I didn't see him again until the next morning, as I was asleep when he came home from the second job.

Jim and I were walking zombies, exhaustion creeping into every cell of our bodies and minds. We needed every bit of energy we could muster to do our jobs of taking care of John and the house, as well as the other kids and our paid work. There was nothing left to give to one another.

After John died, we faced an empty nest far sooner than we thought. The other kids were already out of the house and John's death hastened the fact that none of our kids were living at home any longer. Jim had lost his job with the bank years before John got sick. His job at the post office was half the salary the bank paid, so he got a second job at the church as a bookkeeper. After John died, our debt was such that he still needed the second job to try to pay down our obligations. We considered claiming bankruptcy, but I didn't want to saddle us with a bad credit score and an inability to take out a loan if we needed a car or home appliance.

It is an understatement that we had lost touch with one another and grew apart. We were really nothing but roommates sharing living space. The other enormous problem we had was being able to share our grief over losing John. We were both in mind-numbing pain. It was just impossible for me to think I could share this with Jim because I knew I couldn't help him. My grief was all consuming and so large I just couldn't even hear about how he was feeling. I was completely full of sadness. I couldn't add to it by worrying about his grief. A good marriage is based on constant communication about our feelings, desires, hopes, dreams, and fears. Jim and I found out that we were just unable to communicate our feelings about this horrible loss with one another.

After years of living in this desert of loneliness, I decided I needed to step away for a while. In addition to grief, I was also dealing with lots of anger, disappointment, and frustration with Jim and the terrible state of our marriage. I hated that I had those negative feelings, but they were constantly flashing neon in my mind. I wasn't really thinking about divorce, but I knew I needed time and space apart from my marriage so I could try to understand myself and my feelings. I got an apartment and moved out.

It was an extremely difficult year. I felt guilty for leaving Jim, even if it was just for a while. I had no idea who I was anymore. I lost my child. It was looking like I lost my marriage. I was having a tough time at my job and with my other relationships. I felt so disoriented and adrift. For most of my life, I always knew who I was and what I was supposed to be doing. God had blessed me with five beautiful children. I was content in my chosen vocation as a wife and mother. But the time came when the kids were gone, our marriage didn't behave like a marriage, and everything I thought I was about had changed.

After my one-year lease was up, I asked Dot if I could move in with her for a while. I knew I didn't want to keep the apartment and was leaning toward trying to fix things with Jim and go home. But I wasn't quite ready yet. I painted her rooms upstairs in her house and I asked my boys to help me move there. It was during my time at Dot's house that I realized I no longer felt angry with Jim. Our marriage still needed a lot of work, but I felt calmer and more hopeful that maybe we could fix what was broken and I could go home.

I called Jim and asked him if he would agree to counseling in the hopes that we could get back together. He, of course, did, and after months of intense counseling, I was ready to come home.

Obviously, since this is my book, Jim's perspective is not found here. I have left out the specific things that caused some of my anger because he is not able to share his side of the story. Suffice it to say, in addition to the shared trauma, we had different perspectives on our roles and responsibilities as husband and wife, and often saw the same event in a different way. Healing came when we were finally able to communicate these differences, work through them, and come up with a compromise.

On April 15, 2024, we celebrated forty-six years of marriage. It's not perfect and it's still damn difficult at times. But we continue to help each other be the best person they can be. We fondly remember the good memories and don't dwell on the bad ones. We forgive, cut each other slack for some of our annoying habits, we work harder at communicating, and we show our love in action.

CHAPTER 29

Hello from Heaven

I AM A FIRM BELIEVER in life after death. I believe that this life on earth is not the end of us—that we live on after we die in another perfect place with God and our loved ones. First and foremost, my faith in God that I have nurtured since I was very young supports this belief. I believe in the Bible as being God's Word, and I absolutely know that every word that Jesus spoke is the truth.

Secondly, I have read hundreds of books on near-death experiences (NDEs). These are real accounts of people who had been pronounced clinically dead by an accident, during surgery or some other type of catastrophe. Their experiences are remarkably similar to one another, having many of the same elements, such as moving through a tunnel toward a bright light, feeling more peaceful than they have ever felt in their lives, seeing deceased loved ones, having a life review, not wanting to come back but being told it wasn't their time yet, and other scenes. The first NDE was recorded in France around 1740. Much research has gone into this phenomenon through the centuries, and very recently many scientists are coming around to acknowledge that life does not end when our bodies are clinically dead. Consciousness survives the death of the body. The essence of who we are, our mind, our soul, our specific character traits and memories, travels to a new place, leaving our body behind and experiencing a new existence that is more beautiful, peaceful, and perfect than we could have ever imagined.

And thirdly, John has shown us some very clear signs that he continues to live in another realm, keenly aware of us and our lives. I believe as strongly as I trust that the sun rises each day that John will be waiting for me in heaven and might even be the one to take me by the hand on my deathbed and guide me there.

The following are five experiences that have happened to people close to me that reinforce my belief that Heaven is real, and John lives on there until we are reunited again.

My Sister Patty

The phone rang once at 11 a.m. on a September Saturday morning, only three months after John had passed. I went to pick up the phone, but the caller had already hung up. I checked the caller ID and the number displayed was my sister's. Wondering why Patty would begin to call me and then hang up, I dialed her back. When she answered the phone, I asked her if everything was OK and she said yes, but she had been up since 4 a.m. that morning and was stunned by a dream she had. She had hung up because she had lost her nerve, worrying that I wouldn't believe her. Patty proceeded to tell me about her dream, but she described it as more like a vision because the detail was so real. She said she was on the beach and met John. He was tall, with full dark brown hair, freckles, wearing a t-shirt and shorts and was radiant with health. He looked nothing like the frail, cancer-ravaged teen who had died in June. However, when she looked into his eyes, she recognized that it was indeed John. He greeted Patty and asked her to give me a message. He said, "Please tell my mom that I have arrived on the beach. I am all better and everything is wonderful here. Nothing bad ever happens in this beautiful place. Tell her that I am so grateful that she took such good care of me when I was sick and that I will always watch over her and help her while she is still on earth. Tell her when she misses me, she just needs to close her eyes and go to the beach, and I will be there." The beach was John's favorite place. When he was undergoing an uncomfortable or painful medical procedure, I would tell him to close his eyes and imagine being at the beach. I would describe for him the heat of the soft sand, the whooshing cadence of the ocean waves slapping the coast, the pungent fragrance of salt and sunscreen, and the caw of the seagulls. I would continue to describe for him the brilliant blue sky filled with white wispy clouds and the roar of the planes flying, pulling banners advertising a restaurant or amusement park or other entertainment on the boardwalk. John had a lot of unpleasant procedures, so I used this guided meditation very frequently. It is no coincidence to me that John would describe Heaven as the beach. I truly believe he was there and wanted me to know.

Jim

Dot and I had gone to Ocean City the August after John passed. It was just a short girls' trip to ease and comfort our broken hearts. Jim called me one morning while I was away and proceeded to tell me this dream. "I was in a school building, and I saw John walking toward me. He was tall and handsome and looked completely healthy. I said 'John, what are you doing here? I thought you died.' John answered: 'Dad, I did but I am doing really well. It's wonderful in this place. But don't worry about me, you need to get up now and go to work.' At that precise moment, my alarm clock rang to get me up for work."

Colleen

The Wednesday night before Thanksgiving I was waiting for the kids to come home from college for the holiday. One by one they arrived home, and we hung out in the kitchen for dinner. After we had eaten, we started to discuss where we might want to go for vacation during the summer. Our family tradition was to go to Ocean City for a week. We have been doing this since Katie was a baby. It was the highlight of our year! However, it was everyone's opinion that it might be too sad for us to go to the beach so soon after John's passing. Maybe we needed to change things up and go somewhere completely different. We batted around a couple of ideas and finally settled on spending a week at Deep Creek Lake in western Maryland. We discussed renting a big house there and a pontoon boat for the week. With that settled, the kids dispersed and went out for the evening with their friends, and Jim and I spent a quiet night at home. The next morning the phone rang, and it was Colleen, John's nurse at Hopkins. She apologized for calling me on a holiday but felt an urgency to tell me of the dream she had about John. She proceeded to tell me that she was out somewhere and ran into John, who was organizing play with a bunch of kids and their go-carts. They looked like they were having a marvelous time and John was full of glee as he helped the kids ride. He looked like he was glowing with health and vitality. Colleen said to John: "John, it's so good to see you. You look great!" She went on: "But your mom and dad are having a hard time. They are sad and they miss you so much!" To which John, rather astonishingly said: "Oh, they will be fine. They are going to Deep Creek Lake for vacation this year." No one knew of the conversation that the kids, Jim, and I had had the previous night. We hadn't talked to Colleen since John's death, and she knew nothing of our plans for vacation.

Mary

Mary and Jim, our lifelong dear friends, were the parents of nine amazing children. They brought them up in the Catholic faith, following many of the traditional prayers and services, and always took them to mass. After John had passed, one of their daughters decided on her own to pray a novena (nine days of prayer) to St. Therese the Little Flower. Tradition is that if you make a novena to St. Therese for a particular intercession, you will know that your prayer has been answered by the sign of red roses. In other words, if you ask St. Therese for a miracle or favor, you will know your favor has been granted if red roses appear unexpectedly from a source that is out of the ordinary. Mary's daughter asked St. Therese to show her that John was in Heaven. Some of Mary's children were younger than John and they were of course struggling with his death. The last day of the novena came. Meanwhile, Mary's youngest daughter was suffering from shingles. She was only six years old and was miserable with this illness. Mary's oldest daughter decided to bring her home a present to comfort her. She chose to buy a dozen red roses for her little sister and brought them home to her. Mary asked her why she chose roses as a gift. Surely a coloring book, stuffed animal, or other toy might have been more appropriate. She answered she didn't really know why she chose the flowers. She just felt that was the right gift. The daughter who prayed to St. Therese walked in after school and saw the roses on the counter and stammered, "Where did they come from?" Mary explained, and her daughter knew her prayer had been answered.

My Sister-in-Law Barb

In 2008, my son Ben was ten years old and in fifth grade. He had been suffering from tics and they had been getting progressively worse throughout the school year. He saw a specialist at Hopkins and was diagnosed with Tourette syndrome. He tried various medications to help curb the tics, but they made him very drowsy and put him in a fog-like state.

During spring break, his tics seemed to really spike and he was embarrassed to be around people and didn't want to continue the meds because he hated the way they made him feel.

He said he didn't want to return to school after break and asked me to home-school him.

The day before school resumed, he woke up and said it felt like his tics were not totally gone but much less severe. He told me he prayed to Johnny the night before, asking him to take away his tics. Since then, the tics have been few and far between.

John has never visited me in a dream or in any other way. Maybe it would be too unsettling and sad for me, or make me yearn for him to come back to me even more than I do now. For many years, I asked him to come to me so I could see him again and hear his voice. How I have longed for just a short visit—a second or two to just lay my eyes on him as he is now—healthy and strong and vibrantly alive! But for whatever reason, I have yet to even dream about him. I have had dreams about him, but he is just a baby, or he is sick and ravaged by disease. I even toyed with the idea of getting software that could render an image of John as he might look like now, the kind that the police department uses when they are looking for missing children. But currently, I am content with the dreams that others have had about him as my sign that he indeed is healthy and happy in Heaven and waiting for our reunion. And when I die and enter Heaven, I only want to hear two things—"Well done, good and faithful servant" and "Hi Mom!"

Chapter 30

What If?

I WOULD IMAGINE THAT at one time or another, every person has asked the question, "What if?" What if I had gone to college instead of going right out to work after high school graduation? What if I had married my high school sweetheart instead of my present spouse? What if I had made more money? What if I hadn't made that life-changing decision during my youth? What if I had gone on that trip? What if I had flown on September 11, 2001?

I have asked that question many times. What if I had gone to a four-year college for a specific career? What if I had been able to make more money and save for my retirement? What if John had never gotten sick? What if my daughters hadn't become addicts? What if we had declared bankruptcy during John's catastrophic illness? If these things had or hadn't happened the way they did, would my life have turned out differently? Would my life have been easier?

Yes! Of course, yes! My life would look completely different today had I not suffered through the trials and worst nightmares a parent must ever face. Would I be as happy as I am today? Would I have the confidence I possess now to face anything life throws at me? Would I be at peace with the person I have become and continue to become? I can demonstratively shout an unequivocable: No! I emphatically believe that I am who I am because I have walked the crooked road, the one on which no one wants to travel. It is precisely the broken pieces of that road that have led me to wisdom, understanding, clear insight, and good judgment about life's true meaning and the reason I was born. I could never have learned the tidbits of knowledge I have expressed in this book had I not experienced the anguish found in the trenches of life's battles.

I miss John so much and of course I wish he was still with me. I still cannot make sense of a young child becoming ill and dying. I do not believe for one second that God made this tragedy happen, that He needed John more than I needed him, or that it was part of His perfect plan. It doesn't sound like a perfect plan to cause such suffering in someone you supposedly love. John got sick because the world is flawed, and bad stuff happens. God had nothing to do with causing such pain and agony. But He did make blessings come from such sorrow in the hundreds of lives my young courageous son inspired.

Chrissy and Katie have said many times that they are grateful for their addiction. Because they hit the bottom of the muck in which they were living, they searched for a way out, and that way became a relationship with God and the twelve-step program. They both attended Catholic schools for twelve years and learned their faith expression. But that education wasn't what helped them when they succumbed to their disease and became slaves to their drugs. God literally reached His hand down to help them out of the mire of their addictions and introduced them to good people in recovery who would accompany them into a new life of peace and freedom. But they had to want a life without addiction. They had to admit that they could not manage their lives without the help of God. They had to let go of everything and put themselves in God's hands. Then God suddenly became real to them as they worked through the twelve steps and discovered a newfound love for themselves and others. My daughters now constantly extend their hands to those suffering addictions and help them find a new way through God and His love.

My children and my grandchildren are one of my greatest joys in life! My children grew up to be stunning adults who work hard to take care of their families. They are loving and forgiving and will drop everything if one of them is in trouble. My kids are the best of friends! In a world where families are splintered and siblings and parents are often estranged, my kids treasure each other as family and see each other often. They lend support to each other when needed and celebrate life's joyous events together. Every July, Jim and I and all the kids and grandchildren vacation together at the beach. It's the best week of the year and I revel in the joy of being among my cherished family!

I have been living a very ordinary life in the same little house with the same person for forty-six years. Jim and I have had to hold off retirement because we cannot yet afford it. We are still in debt from the years of extraordinary medical expenses but are slowly paying it down by working part-time jobs. We don't travel or enjoy many luxuries but are comfortable and our needs are met. I used to carry resentments over not being able to afford a bigger home with our large family or get the latest in technology that would help make our lives easier. I was jealous of so many of our retired peers being able to take new adventures and go to places I've never been. I am sobered into accepting the fact that, at this stage in my life, I will never know what it feels like to have enough money to pay all my bills. But I hear there is no such thing as having enough money—apparently the temptation is to spend as much money as we make, therefore completing the never-ending cycle of earning and spending and then earning more and spending more.

What I have now is more precious, more valuable, and more satisfying than a bigger house, the newest gadgets, or an exciting trip to an exotic place. I have the answer to "how to be happy"! I will never be happy if I constantly compare myself to others who have more. I am comparing myself to the wrong others! I need to see my blessings in relation to others who have much less or who are impoverished physically, mentally, emotionally, or spiritually and be humbly grateful for what I have. And then I take the next step and try to ease the burden of others who have less. I have quite dramatically learned that happiness occurs when I am grateful for what I have and serve others to give them what they need.

I am certainly not perfect and work hard correcting my character flaws with God's help. Sometimes I find myself enjoying the occasional pity party when I am down. I own my emotions, talk to someone I trust about them, and then push the reset button to get back on track. Life is hard. There is no doubt about it. I learned the hard way that to expect life to go your way and shower you with only good things is a delusion. I know there are more trials in the future I will have to face, and I certainly don't look forward to suffering through them. But I have no fear about what's ahead. I know God walks beside and within me every day. I give my life to Him every morning and thank Him every night. And when the road gets rough, He will carry me as He has done so many times in the past.